Bitter Harvest in the Promised Land

Myths, History and Conflict

Inge Etzbach

I0409583

Bitter Harvest in the Promised Land

Promised Land

Myths, History and Conflict

Inge Etzbach

Bitter Harvest in the Promised Land
Myths, History and Conflict
Inge Etzbach

This book was published before under the title:
"In the Land of Milk and Honey – the Struggle in the Jewish Soul"

ISBN-13: 978-1489588524

ISBN-10: 1489588523

Pluto Press, 345 Archway Road, London N6 5AA, UK, www.plutobooks.com, gave permission to quote material from the book "The Myth of Zionism" by John Rose, Published 2004

Printed in the United States of America

Almvillabooks

almvillabooks.weebly.com

almvillabooks@gmail.com

$12.95

Previously published:

Reflections at Sundown
Looking back at what really mattered

Growing up before Yesterday
Memory of a Time Gone with the Wind

Beyond Truth
Collections of Essays and Observations

Elie Wiesel

Dedication

To all activists who translate their passionate craving for decency into work promoting justice for all human beings.

Special thanks to Marjorie Wright, Ricky Bernstein, Lisa Sheble, Anne Landsfield, Jan Hutchison, Fanny Prizant who read the working proofs and gave me advice and encouragement. Their support was invaluable to me. Also thanks to my daughter, Rev. Stefanie Etzbach-Dale, who was with me all the time even though my political interests clashed with her spiritual endeavours.

Contents

Introduction

This book is the product of an extraordinary, life-long obsession: my deep sorrow for the pain caused by the Holocaust; my compassion for its victims, Jewish and later Palestinian, usually referred to as Arabs; my love for the land, raw and beautiful and full of traces of human history and struggle, and my desire to find out the reasons, the forces, the inevitable flow of history and faith, and even the results of errors and human failings. All of these bring us to the tragedy we are confronted with today. The book is also influenced by the prophetic words of those people who try to find ways to heal the wounds of their country and its inhabitants.

There are two different narratives: The Jews speak about the Holocaust, the 20th century genocide which aimed to kill them all, after centuries of living in nations and countries among people who saw them as outsiders. It was their desire to have a country of their own where the word "Jew" was not an insult, and that country was to be in Palestine. A 19th century movement called Zionism worked towards that goal.

The other narrative, that of the Palestinians, speaks about "The Naqba", the Catastrophe, during which this Jewish homeland was established on the land which had been owned and settled by them for centuries. Hundreds of thousands of their people were driven into refugee camps and subjected to suppression, incarceration and contemptuous treatment. They are fighting back and are called terrorists, when in effect they see themselves as freedom fighters.

Both narratives are painful and speak of deep suffering, but it is not helpful to grade these two kinds of suffering as to severity. The memory of the Holocaust is tremendously painful to the Jews, but the Naqba, the dislocation and expulsion of the Palestinians from their people's land and the subsequent life under the heavy hand of occupiers is also a heavy painful burden.

My question is: why do the children of the Holocaust who have suffered the depth of despair and cruelty themselves, treat another people with such colonial disregard and lack of empathy? This book tries to explain the mindset of Jews and the culture of their past in the hope that it will provide the Palestinians with greater understanding. While there seems to be greater willingness on the side of the Palestinians to cooperate and co-exist, the Zionists are relying on "absolute truths" which are represented as historical facts in the Torah and bolster and undergird the Jews' claim to the land in Palestine as unquestioned rights.

Jews themselves might benefit from examining their history and the events and interpretations of their old tribal and religious beliefs which are supporting their worldview. They may gain a larger and more universal understanding by listening to the insights of eminent Jewish scholars which clarify reasons and assumptions. The requirement is having an open mind.

The Holocaust has been a terrible burden on my soul for my teenage and adult years. It has never let me go and influenced many decisions. I was wrestling with a very fundamental problem, namely how to live morally, even heroically, in a random, indifferent universe. I see the key to a lot of the conflicts, problems and misunderstandings in the world as the tendency to look for the Truth with a capital T. This leads us to adhere to a viewpoint we think of as absolutely true and an unshakable interpretation of the events and situations in the world according to this immutable truth. Questions like: Did Abraham really bring Monotheism to Canaan, and did God really promise Canaan to his son Isaak? Did God really make a covenant with Moses on Mount Sinai and make the Jews His chosen people? Did He give the land of Canaan to the Jews? What is the origin of the Jewish people and how did the Jewish religion develop? Did King David ever have a large Jewish kingdom in Jerusalem? Are all of these stories History or Myths?

Believers will find comfort in a religion which developed its expression after the events of its formation. Judaism embodies the ethical and moral structure of the Western world and as such is untouchable. But Zionism is built on "historical facts" as written down in the Torah,

3

when it has become clear that "This land is ours – God gave us this Land – We are God's Chosen people" needs examination. I hope to make people aware of the value of doubt and make them ask themselves: "Can she possibly have a point there?"

In Praise of Doubt
By Rev. Richard S. Gilbert
From his book "In the Holy Quiet of this Hour"

It is not that we are not believers.
It is that our belief
Has to be passed through the fires of skepticism
And boiled in the crucible of doubt.

You have heard it said,

"Ours is not to reason why,
Ours is but to do and die."

But I say unto you,

Ours is not to doubt and die,
Ours is to seek the reason why.

When we doubt, we affirm the importance of reason
And our confidence in ourselves as centers of religious authority.
When we doubt, we affirm the seriousness of the religious quest.
When we doubt, we recognize that truth was not engraved in stone
2,000 years ago.
When we doubt, we acknowledge that our understanding of truth is
imperfect.
When we doubt, we strengthen our faith.

This is to thank all those scientists, scholars, political thinkers, writers and truth searchers, on all sides of the issues, who over the years have dealt – courageously - with the subjects which are my own passionate interest. It was their vision, their deep understanding, their discoveries, convictions and rejections which gave me the courage to delve into this difficult subject matter myself. Thousands of books have been written. I cannot touch on every subject. All I can do is examine the red line which took me on a journey from Canaan and a collection of oral tales and myths to the Bible-as-History, then finally leading to Zionism and the creation of a Jewish State of Israel on questionable foundations. In conclusion, I believe we must contemplate what avenues can be taken to heal the wounds of those people who live in the land where milk and honey flows.

I had no one to ask for advice in the process of writing this book, so all mistakes, errors and misconceptions are entirely my own. It is impossible to do justice to all relevant subjects and ideas in a slim volume more suited to a broad overview. This book is meant to guide readers to other, more in-depth resources and to greater understanding of the complex issues at work in an area that calls for reason, compassion and a careful balance between the longing of one's soul and the need to consider the souls of others.

My Story

Witnessing, as a 12-year old child, American troops liberating a Concentration Camp and seeing the emaciated inmates in striped prison uniforms stream out of the gates, was the defining event of my life. I had started the day as a fully indoctrinated Nazi child, drilled in school and twice-weekly Hitler Youth meetings. I even became a leader of a small group of girls. We were required to chant slogans in unison, such as: "I am nothing – my people are everything!" or "Fuehrer, command us – we will obey you!", and we saluted often. I had taken in the ideology like any indoctrinated child, no matter what ideology. That is why I, who had never met a Jew in person, hated all Jews with a vengeance. And I hated and despised with the same intensity Russians, Poles, blacks, retarded people, handicapped people - inferior or worthless life, as they were called.

But that afternoon I was standing at the front door, shaking, crying, looking at the endless stream of pitiful humanity, of men hardly able to walk yet supporting others even sicker - dehumanized men who still had the compassion to care about others. What I had considered inferior and worthless life before, I saw now as suffering, broken-down human beings capable of more decency and kindness than anybody I knew, and I swore that, in the future, I would never, ever believe anything anybody told me without checking it out first, that I would never, ever follow any doctrine, political or religious, without making sure that it was based on Truth, and that I would never, ever follow any man without the most critical analysis of his character and message. The Holocaust, the defining event in my own life, extends my concerns to all suppressed and oppressed minorities and therefore also to the fate of the Palestinians. The horrors of such mass brutality must never again happen to Jews, but they must also not happen to people of any other religious, racial, ethnic or national origin. The roots of conflict demand attention.

Starting from this conviction and my later personal experiences in Israel, on a Kibbutz, as a Volunteer for Israel on an Israeli army base cleaning Uzi guns, hitchhiking through the country and immersing myself in its history, culture and people, I moved into awareness of the deeper political realities of the Palestinian question and into the burning need to know why the children of the Holocaust, who had suffered the depth of despair and cruelty themselves, would treat another people with such colonial disregard and lack of compassion.

For many years I carried the burden of the Holocaust on my shoulders. But then, on one of my trips to Israel and Palestine I was sitting at a café in the Old City of Jerusalem and overheard a group of Israelis and Americans, obviously Jews, at the next table speak about Arabs. One of them said: "One should line them all up against the wall and mow them down with submachine guns!" I sat there, ice cold and shaken, and finally got up, went over to their table, identified myself as German and pointed out that my people had actually done to Jews what they were proposing to do to Arabs, and did they really mean it? There was a deep silence, and finally one of them apologized and said he had not been thinking and he was sorry. It was only then that I realized that evil lurks in the souls of people of all nations and religions, and I was finally able to let go of the idea of a specific, unshakeable German character flaw. That burden was replaced by the knowledge of sharing in a larger, more universal truth, namely a responsibility for all humanity.

What are the reasons underlying the current Israeli/Palestinian crisis? Can one blame the Palestinians for defending their land "by any means necessary?" Did the founders of Zionism know about the certain conflict between Jews and Arabs and proceed anyway? Do the recent

9

archeological discoveries in the West Bank, questioning the Exodus and the Kingdom of David as facts, undermine the "Jewish Right to the Land of Israel"? Do recent findings regarding the origin of the Israelites and the evolution of God create any doubt regarding viewing the Bible as built on myths, not necessarily history?

I believe that the search for pragmatic solutions to any political problem requires the examination, with honesty and openness, of the ingrained mindsets and worldviews of the parties involved. I started by examining the unquestioned assumptions underlying the Jewish historical and biblical convictions, going back to the Bronze Age in Canaan. and questioned by biblical scholars and eminent archeologists after they were able to enter the West Bank for excavations after the Six-Day War in 1967.

After living on a kibbutz and on an army base and staying in youth hostels during my travels, for the last night I rented a room at the Intercontinental Hotel on the Mount of Olives in Jerusalem. My room overlooked the Old City of Jerusalem, the Temple Mount with the golden Dome of the Rock and the adjacent City of David, and to the left I could see Bethlehem in the distance. Further to the right lay the ancient city of Jericho. I sat at the window from noon of one day to noon of the next, through dusk and night and dawn, while reading the myths and historical narratives of the Old Testament from cover to cover and feasting my eyes on this incomparable sight. Many of the events described in the Bible happened right there in front of me. The history of Israel is one of epic proportions. Power, conquests and

10

occupation, weakness and loss, constant growth and decay, ever-present change symbolizes the history of this land. Peace only reigned for short periods of time. Then the balance of power shifted and internal or external pressure led to a new political arrangement: to a (in the final analysis) temporary solution. The Old City of Jerusalem before my window was conquered 38 times through history, and every conquest was devastating for the residents, inconceivable in its implications. Is it possible that, seen in the grand sweep of history, the Jewish State of Israel is only another episode like many others before? Reading, as I did, of the events spanning 4000 years related in the Bible and seeing before me the very places where they are said to have occurred, I could not help but see the current existence of Israel as an episode, a passing phase, one more heartbreaking historical event like so many before, only one event in a chain of events reaching from the distant past into the future. Time will roll on and somehow, in some fashion, life will go on and arrange itself until that arrangement in turn will be put to the test. Change, like life and death, growth and decay, is the only constant in history. And all we humans can do is work for justice.

> "The arc of the moral universe is long, but it bends toward justice."

> Theodore Parker

11

Myths and Interpretations

THE BIBLE AS HISTORY

For more than 2000 years, the Bible has been the companion, the comforter, the educator, the moral teacher of the Jews and - in later years - the Christians. It has been translated into many languages, copied, quoted and read by innumerable people. It has been issued in different formats, adapted to different times and printed in different editions. For many years it was often the most valuable book a family owned, and frequently the only one. Its influence is impossible to estimate. Wars have been fought over its content and interpretations. Millions of people have lived and died for it because it contained God's word. It has been praised as a great work of religion, of philosophy, of literature and history. Its stories and phrases permeate the texture of Western culture.

To Jews, it recounts their history, their assurance of God's covenant with them, their culture, celebrations, promises and expectations. To be Jewish means to have the Torah define your religion, your history and your sense of self. The Hebrew Bible – i.e. the Bible in Hebrew – is called a work of unique and intoxicating beauty.

The stories of Abraham and Passover, the Exodus, Moses and the Burning Bush, the conquest of Jericho and the Kingdom of David always were and are fundamental to Israelite history and to the self-concept of the Jewish people. They are inextricably linked to the main pillars of the Jewish faith, forming a large part of Jewish culture which would be unthinkable without these events, and politically they are considered proof of the Jewish people's right to a homeland in Palestine..

Doubts arose about the veracity of the Bible quite early, initially in the 11th century. More recently, in the 19th century, Protestant biblical scholars addressed the coherence of the text itself. It was generally understood that it was written by a number of inspired people at different times, was not God's immutable word and, therefore, probably incorporated errors. At the beginning of the 20th century some archeological excavations were undertaken to prove the truth of some of the descriptions in biblical texts, after which books were written to show that "the bible is right after all!" As Israel Finkelstein, the director of the Institute of Archaeology at Tel Aviv University, said: "Biblical history dictated the course of research and archaeology and was used in order to prove the biblical narrative".

14

Archeologists had no access to the West Bank, the ancient land settled by the early Israelites, before Israel conquered the area in the war of 1967. Only after that could they enter and do exploratory excavations of the many tells and ruins, and develop a consistent system of dating pottery shards, coins, house foundations etc. These were often found in many layers, indicating habitation over hundreds and perhaps thousands of years. The resulting findings questioned Biblical truths and caused an uproar in Israel and many discussions as to how they could be interpreted.

Whereas many archeological discoveries may be disregarded because "the absence of evidence is not necessarily evidence of absence", the story of the Exodus is crucial and the archeological findings are compelling.

ABRAHAM

The Book of Genesis contains many myths of Sumerian origins, like the Creation of the Universe, Creation of Man, Paradise, the Flood, Cain/Abel, the Tower of Babel, and the Dispersion of Mankind. These myths were handed on through oral tradition, collected and incorporated in the Bible during the first century BCE. Biblical experts agree that we have no definite knowledge of the existence of Abraham who reportedly lived around 1995 BCE, when writing had not yet developed in Canaan. Many Sumerian tales had been preserved by oral tradition, finding their way eventually into Genesis. Abraham, who was seen as the father of the Arab and Hebrew people via his children Ishmael and Isaac, was considered the first person to realize that there is only one God.

All we know about Abraham is in the Torah – there is no direct evidence of his existence. His name is not found among the Sumerian cuneiform tablets, nor listed on any stele in the Middle East or Egypt.

Modern scholars are extremely skeptical about the historical authenticity of Abraham and Isaac, and it is therefore necessary to approach the story of Abraham with caution. After all, Genesis and the stories in the Torah represent the *Jewish interpretation of events*, set up in such a way that they benefitted Jews and the interests of the Jewish people.

Since all knowledge was handed on orally, it could easily have been *changed and transformed over more than a thousand years of oral transmission.* Genesis relates that, after Abraham came to Canaan, God said: "I will make you into a great nation. I will bless you and make your name famous and you shall be a blessing. Also in you all the families of earth shall be blessed". And, "I am the Lord who brought you from Chaldean Ur to give you this land to possess and to your descendants I will give this country from the river of Egypt to the Great River, the river Euphrates". He also stated that he would establish his covenant between himself and Abraham and his descendents in their successive generations for ever.

Everybody who wants to know what went on with Abraham will go straight to the Bible and will read the *Jewish interpretation,* namely that Abraham was the first monotheist. Yet the voice that calls Abraham is said to belong to Yahweh, whereas he performs circumcision at the request of El Shaddai, and plants a tree on behalf of El Olam. He appears to serve several gods, all without leaving any tangible evidence of his existence, except stories preserved through the efforts of generations of story tellers.

Monotheism is the belief in a single, all-powerful God, the totally self-sufficient creator of the world. In Judaism, Abraham's son Isaac became the father of the Jews, and his other son, Ishmael, the father of the Arabs, setting up a crucial division between the people in the country early on.

If there were never an Abraham, no gift of the Promised Land, no division between the Jews and the Arabs, no covenant between God and the Hebrews as God's Chosen people, what conclusions might this lead to?

EXODUS

The foundation of the entire Bible is resting on the events which are supposed to have taken place in the 13th century BCE when writing was practiced in Egypt but was unknown in Canaan. The Israelite Moses, raised by Pharaoh's sister, led his people out of slavery and persecution in Egypt. He is said to have guided them through the Red Sea and the Sinai desert towards Canaan, conquering Jericho and therefore Canaan itself. The Torah considers the existence of the Israelites in Canaan from the time of the Exodus and bases the Jewish right to the land on this event. Egypt occupied and administered Canaan during the Iron Age II and maintained a number of extensive strongholds. In the ruins of Tel-Armana in upper Egypt, headquarters of the occupation forces in Canaan, about 400 tablets were found describing Cannanite affairs. Neither the exodus nor the existence of a large number of slaves in the home country were mentioned. Neither did any of the other writings in Egypt mention a Moses leading the slaves. No monuments show Israelite slaves escaping in a truly sensational manner: through parting waters which let the slaves through, but killed the Egyptian soldiers in pursuit.

It is very difficult to point to an area in Upper Egypt which would fit the description of parting waters. An exhaustive examination of the topography of the Northern Nile Valley in ancient times does not show any place where the water could have been forded easily. Some experts say that "Red Sea" should read "Reed Sea", but that describes a shallow marshy area which would have bogged down horses and chariots.

The 40 year trek by the Israelites through the Sinai Desert gave rise to a number of theological themes which were important for the foundation of the religion of Yahweh, namely, the establishment of the tabernacle and priesthood, the people's faithlessness and God's punishment, and numerous laws and commandments and regulations. Some of them reflect the viewpoint of a later urban population, not that of desert wanderers. Dozens of towns are listed as the path of the trek. The problem is that many of them did not exist in the 13th century, but had existed before and were already destroyed when the people were said to have passed by, or were built a long time afterwards. Some listed towns were actually Egyptian fortresses and the question arises why these Egyptians let the mass of Israelites enter the country. Another known site is "Kadesh-barnea" where Israelites were supposedly quartered for 38 years before they entered Canaan. Extensive archaeological excavations have been undertaken at this place, but not even one potsherd from the 13th century BCE, the time frame for the Exodus, was found. In addition, Kadesh-Barnea is a small tell and would not have been more than a small village at that time, too small to house the large troop of slaves for 38 years. The Bible records that there were 600,000 males aged between 20 and 60. With children and families, that would amount to somewhere between 2½ and 3 million in total. (Exodus 12:37). This large number of travelers poses several questions. For instance, could they be sheltered in a small village for such a long period of time? Furthermore, a group of more than a million people wandering through the Sinai Desert would present an unsolvable logistics problem, given the need for food and water supplies. Manna and quail supplied by God (as per the Bible) would not have sufficed.

The Bible claims that more than fifty sites were conquered. But only a small number of them would even be potential candidates for such Israelite destruction in the period from ca. 1250-1150 BCE. Surprisingly, names are given for all "conquered" sites, but Mount Sinai is not mentioned among them. Josh. 10:40 claims that Joshua annihilated Amorites, Canaanites, Prizzites, Hivites, and Jebusites and had

> "defeated the whole land, the hill country and the Negev and the lowlands and the slopes, and all their kings; he left no one remaining, but destroyed all that breathed, as the Lord God of Israel commanded".

23

According to the Bible, the conquest of Canaan was followed by a conquest of Jericho by the Israelites. Obeying the command of God, the Israelites killed everybody, men and women and children together with all livestock, and destroyed the town.

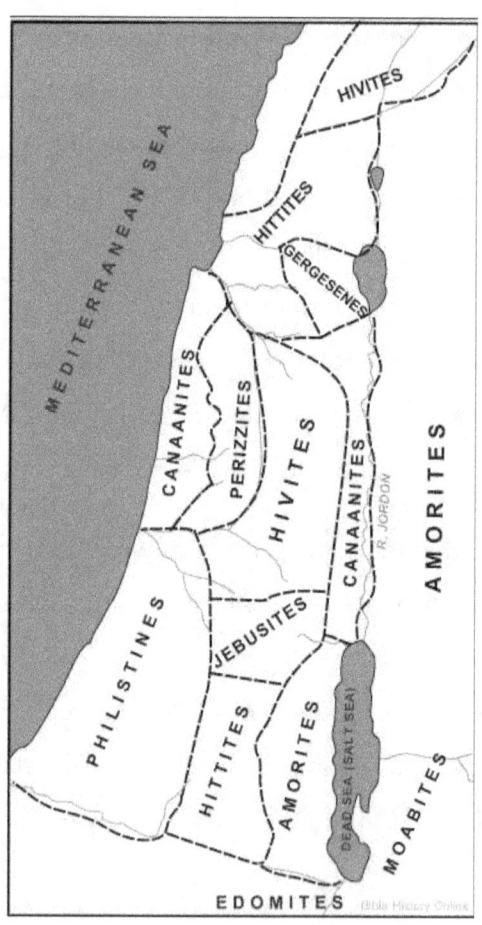

Excavations at Jericho were attempted in the 1920s and showed a massive destruction of mud brick city walls, which seemed to substantiate the biblical story of conquest. The archaeologist Dame Kathleen Kenyon, however, excavated at Jericho between 1955 and 1958 with new and superior methods, proclaiming herself unencumbered by any "biblical baggage". She proved that the destruction shown in the ruins was dated to ca. 1500 BCE and was part of an Egyptian campaign. She also showed, beyond doubt, that during the time period of any Israelite "conquest", Jericho was already completely abandoned. Not one potsherd from that period was found in the entire site, and there is no trace of any Late Bronze Age II occupation.

In October 1999, Prof. Ze'ev Herzog of the University of Tel Aviv's Institute of Archaeology published an article in Ha'aretz entitled: "Deconstructing the Walls of Jericho" (see Attachment). The article, which is disregarded by the fundamentalist Jewish Orthodox, is not widely discussed because it gnaws at the foundations of the Jewish narrative. It makes modern secular Zionists very uncomfortable because it undermines the justification for insisting, based on biblical history, on a homeland for the Jewish people in a land that, besides Israelites, was home for Canaanite Hittites, Amorites, Perizzites, Hivites, Girgashites, Jebusites, Philistines, Ammonites, Moabites, and Edomites who had their own substantial city-states, their own governments, their own God and their own culture.

In 2012 CE Prof. Israel Finkelstein, working on excavations at Meggido, discovered a clay container with precious Canaanite gold jewelry originating from around 1100 BCE. Meggido at that time was a substantial town in the Jezreel Valley. This find shows that other tribes, among whom the Israelites lived, had a high level of development and an urban culture comparable to that of the Israelites in Jerusalem 200 years later. The name Canaan means "Land of Purple" (a purple dye was extracted from a murex shellfish found near the shores of Palestine). The features of many cultures of the ancient Near East were absorbed and assimilated for centuries by the Canaanites even before the Israelites arose as a distinctive tribe. As far as is known, the Canaanites invented the form of writing that later became the alphabet, which was passed on to many cultures and nations through the Greeks and Romans.

DAVID'S KINGDOM

According to the Torah, King David stands as the true founder of the United Kingdom of Israel and the creator of Jerusalem as the political and spiritual nexus of the Israelites. As a young man, David is reported to have captured Jerusalem via a surprise attack up a water chute created by the original owners (the Jebusites) in order to supply water to the city itself from a well outside of the walls. This construction, remnants of which still exist, shows the conceptual and mechanical genius of the Jebusites. Egyptian texts mention Jerusalem first in the 19th to 18th centuries BCE. Various Canaanite sub-kings administered the town for a time during Egyptian rule before the Jebusites arrived. The oldest part of the settlement is the spur, called the hill of Ophel, from the eastern hill of the city which was known as Zion. Scholars suppose that the Jebusites had their stronghold there. The Bible describes David as capturing it, indicating that he "dwelt in the stronghold and called it the City of David".

Again according to the Bible, David's Jerusalem was extended and beautified as his capital. He built a magnificent palace with gold ornaments and precious wood for many wives and hundreds of concubines. He is also credited with having made plans for the first temple. Excavations on the hill of Ophel by the Archaeologist Ronnie Reich showed that findings are either several centuries too early or several centuries too late. The massive blocks of the Western Wall go back in origin to the early Canaanite period of the Middle Bronze Age. One part of the outer wall projected from the City of David is later in date, too late to be ascribed to King David. Findings from the area were from the eighth century BCE, two centuries after the time of David and Solomon. According to Reich, we have evidence only of the Canaanites in the 18th century BCE and the Israelites in the 8th century BCE. In between there is a huge gap without any broken pottery whatsoever. Despite dozens of archaeologists digging and sifting over a period of 150 years, no clear archaeological evidence has been found for King David's capital. Reich thinks that King David's palace "would have been probably only a little bit larger than a private house in modern Jerusalem." Another famous Archaeologist, Israel Finkelstein, said

> "There is almost no evidence for the tenth century. There is almost no evidence for Solomon. Jerusalem at this time was probably a very small village, or a very poor town.
> ....

> Reexamination of the archaeological evidence ... points to a period of a few decades [in which a strong Israel existed] between around 835-800 BCE.[1]"

It seems that Jerusalem only became an important urban center in the 9th century, after the United Monarchy fell apart into the two parts of Samaria and Judea. Jerusalem therefore was never the capital of Israel; it was the capital of Judea, the southern part.

Prof. Dever, true to his principle of examining other opinions and findings, spent a lot of time on investigating claims pertaining to all the settlements on the path of conquest in Canaan, giving due respect to situations that could have been, events that could have happened, and news that could still be discovered. He agrees with other archaeologists that the Exodus and the circumstances regarding David's Kingdom are a matter of epic, not of history, and therefore are questionable.

But King David was not a legend – he did live. In 1939 the Archaeologist Biran found a stone with an inscripton which said: "... king of the house of David" in early Aramaic. It was discovered under a layer of destruction debris dating from the late eighth century BCE .

---

[1] Finkelstein, Israel, and Silberman, Neil Asher "The Bible Unearthed".

29

EXILE AND DIASPORA

The Declaration of the Establishment of the State of Israel reads:

> After being forcibly exiled from their land, the people kept faith
> with it throughout their Dispersion and never ceased to pray and
> hope for their return to it and for the restoration in it of their
> political freedom.

Prof. Shlomo Sands, Professor at Tel Aviv University, is the author of
the book "The Invention of the Jewish People", listed on the Bestseller
List in Israel for 19 months. His goal was to examine the deeply
embedded convictions prevalent among Jewish people, especially the
one that the "Jewish Nation" was forcibly exiled by the Romans after
the fall of the Second Temple in 70 CE, then wandered homeless about
the world for 2,000 years and now has reclaimed the country given by
God (as attested to in the Torah) as a homeland. The creation of the
State of Israel in the 20th century CE is considered by Zionists to be a

non-negotiable right, an assumption of course not shared by the Palestinians, the other occupants of the land.

The forcible deportation and exile of the Jews after the destruction of the first Temple in 585 BCE was a devastating experience, never to be forgotten. The character of Judaism developed and was formed during the subsequent exile. After 50 years the refugees were allowed to go back home, but as Mr. Sand noted, not all came back to Judaea – quite a number settled in Mesopotamia and stayed there and even went further afield, founding other Jewish towns. There were large Jewish settlements outside of Judaea even before the Babylonian exile. In fact, the Temple in Jerusalem was a pilgrimage destination for all those Jews who lived in other countries.

Also explained in detail by John Rose in *The Myths of Zionism*, there were three main groups of Jews in the country itself, not one united nation; those living in Judaea with its center of Jerusalem and the Temple, the Samaritans who called themselves Jewish but were not accepted and were even enemies of the Judaean Jews, and the Jews in Galilee who were more independent and did not join in the Judaean revolt against Rome. Ever since Alexander the Great's conquest established a universal empire in the 4th century BCE, a Jewish Diaspora began to Egypt and other countries surrounding the Mediterranean, so that by the first century of the Common Era, "the majority of Jews were living outside Judaea."[2] The First Jewish Revolt

---

[2] Barclay, J.M.G. *Jews in the Mediterranean Diaspora)*

32

against the Romans from 66 – 73 CE was really a revolt of the peasant Jews against the very wealthy Jewish ruling class in Jerusalem and also against Rome itself. It resulted, as Josephus Flavius wrote in his book, in the destruction of the Second Temple and the killing and enslavement of many people in and around Jerusalem. They were sometimes forced to vacate their farms and leave their homes, but in no way can one speak of the deportation of the whole population. Romans were ruthless in their warfare, but they did not drive away farmers and workers who were necessary to maintain their economy.

The Bar Kochbar Revolt 60 years later resulted in the law that henceforth no Jew was allowed to live in Jerusalem itself. Many Jews migrated to the Galilee and over the years found their way even to China and India. This law caused great upheaval in the observance of Judaism which traditionally had found its focus in the Temple and now, for the sake of the continuity of the religion under different circumstances, needed to find a way to build an observance without the necessity of guidance by the temple priests.

In order to provide for a continuation of the faith without access to the Temple and the acts of sacrifice, the rabbinical priesthood worked to develop texts, stories and rituals, all centered on synagogues and family life and not tied to presence in the Temple. Myths were forged into historical facts. The religion could now be practiced anywhere. Weekly candle lighting, seders, special food, stories, feast days and customs, all tied to historical myths, connection to God and promises of the return to the land, repeated again and again, formed a strong emotional bond within the Jewish communities wherever they lived and sustained the religion through centuries.

Jerusalem itself, deprived of its life blood, deteriorated after that, and large numbers of Jews emigrated to other countries and established viable communities in North Africa, Libya, Cyprus, and Alexandria and further on in Rome and Marseilles. Evidence was found in rabbinical texts that in the 2nd and 3rd centuries of the Common Era, the term "galut" (exile) was used in the sense of political subjugation instead of deportation and that the renewed Jewish idea of exile was actually developed by Christians as punishment for the Jew's rejection and crucifixion of Jesus. "Exile" denoted an existential situation which could exist anywhere.[3]

It is obvious that people have always mixed, moved and settled in foreign countries, married foreign women, and have left behind children to carry their genes into future generations. The earth was populated over millennia by people who left their old homes and found a new ones. Some of these migrations resulted from a change of weather conditions, under the force of occupation by foreign troops, or by a search for better living conditions in a world increasingly populated and competitive. This is evident from the number of Jews who have made their home in all countries around the world. The United States, for instance, counts within its borders more Jews than

---

[3] Sands, Shlomo *The Invention of the Jewish People*, pg 133

the State of Israel itself has, and they make a home here and promote their own welfare together with the welfare of the country. There is obviously no great attempt made by them to return to the land which, according to tradition, God gave them as their own.

Culture and Religion

THE ORIGIN OF THE HEBREWS

Archaeologists on the full spectrum of positions, political or otherwise, do agree that there is no evidence of a forceful conquest of Jericho and Canaan. External material evidence supplies no proof whatsoever of the biblical account of a large-scale and determined invasion of Israelites into Canaan. We now know that the stories about military conquest are later literary inventions, partly for theological reasons. But where did the early Israelites come from? William G. Dever in his book *Who Were the Early Israelites and Where Did They Come From?* lists several basic approaches to evaluate the discoveries.

1. One can assume that the biblical text is *literally* true and ignore all external evidence as irrelevant (fundamentalist approach), or
2. Reject the text and any other data, since the Bible *cannot* be true (minimalist approach).

Dever himself goes the middle road, namely "approach the text, as well as the external data, with *no preconceptions.* Single out the 'convergences' of the two lines of evidence, and remain skeptical about the rest." It is this approach which he uses in his book and which carefully evaluates the details.

There is general agreement that there was a slow takeover, rather than a conquest. Here are several models of peaceful infiltration:

Dr. Adam Zertal of the University of Haifa is convinced, from his surveys and the examination of pottery finds, that there was a gradual move westward over the Jordan by Bedouins who settled in the mountain range running down the length of Canaan. Others consider that questionable, since Bedouins who are used to deserts and tents, do not settle down easily, preferring nomadic life.

Another explanation might be that, in response to a wide-spread drought in the Mediterranean area during the Late Bronze/Early Iron Age, peasants were driven out of farmland in the low-lying areas along the seashore and migrated to the hilly spine running from North to South through the land of Canaan. In addition, between 1200 and

1176 BCE, the so-called "Sea People" invaded and settled along the Mediterranean, causing wide-spread chaos in the region that forced inhabitants of that area to flee into the less accessible mountains.

Another model would be based on "withdrawal" of certain Canaanites called *Hiberu* or *Apiro* into the hill country to avoid contact with other tribes. These people, variously described as "nomadic or semi-nomadic, rebels, outlaws, raiders, mercenaries, bowmen, servants, slaves, migrant laborers, etc." were reported in a 14th century BCE letter from the king of the Canaanite city-state of Shechem to his Egyptian overlord. The word *Hebrew* has been associated with the words *Hiberu* or *Apiru*, described as the name given by various Sumerian, Egyptian, Akkadian, Hittite, Mitanni and Ugaritic sources (from before 2500 BCE to around 1200 BCE) to a group of people in areas from Mesopotamia and Iran to Egypt and Canaan. The Hiberu seem to have been more a social class than an ethnic group, living as itinerant people at the outer edges of civilization, contributing to political instability. Why were these people nomads and outlaws, clinging to the outer edges of society, trying to scrounge out a living? In 1628 BCE, an earthquake on the island of Santorini brought the Minoan civilization to an end, collapsing most of the island itself and sending a huge tsunami all along the Eastern shore of the Mediterranean, destroying settlements, changing weather patterns and causing political and economic disruption and one of the largest migrations on record. The resulting chaos and insecurity might be a reason for the formation of an underclass of "dropouts."

39

Archaeologists cannot easily prove the social movements in the distant past, but they know from their excavations that a wave of new settlements appeared in the previously uninhabited Middle East during the Bronze Age. They were similar to existing settlements, but different in one aspect: the inhabitants of the new settlements did not eat pork since no pork bones were found. One of the excavations showed that these people might have had some idea of a precursor of Yahweh, but were still venerating the Canaanite god El, just like their Canaanite neighbors. After all, "Isra-El" means "fighter for El".

It is an accepted assumption that the ancient Israelites were not conquerors and immigrants from other parts of the country, bringing their fully-formed god Yahweh with them, but part of the indigenous inhabitants of Canaan venerating Canaanite gods. According to Jon Entine, author of *Abraham's Children – Race, Identity, and the DNA of the Chosen People[4]*, DNA research by Dr. Ariella Oppenheim of Hebrew University has shown that "seven out of ten Jewish men and half of Arab men whose DNA was studied inherited their male chromosomes from the same paternal ancestors, who lived in the prehistoric Middle East during the Neolithic Period, about 7,800 years ago." They have about 18% of their chromosomes in common, showing a genetic closeness from prehistoric times, but little intermixing since the establishment of their respective communities. This affirms the scientific findings that the Israelites started out as part of the

---

[4] Page 332

indigenous inhabitants of Canaan and have their roots in the same population that brought forth the Palestinians and other Middle Eastern peoples.

THE EVOLUTION OF YAHWEH

Current scholars see the emergence of Israelite monotheism as a gradual process which began with the normal beliefs and practices of the ancient world. It is impossible to say with any kind of certainty how the gods of a number of small tribes in the Middle East of 3000 years ago developed and evolved, merged and changed, and finally ended up as a single god (perhaps with the DNA of other minor gods, and perhaps with the characteristics and myths of others). Everything happened when there was yet no writing. Stories were transmitted orally. But even later, when all these stories were collected and put into writing as parts of the Bible, they passed through the minds and belief systems of scribes, who were influenced by politics, wishful thinking, hopeful adaptation and *interpretation*. So the Bible actually contains a jumble of impressions and tales.

The stories in the Torah, written down during the first millennium, contain various names for the God in question. There are the names

43

El and Elyon and Elohim, El Shaddai, Yahweh and Adonai, sometimes in the same verse and sometimes in the same sentence. The Hebrew word "El" is like the English word "God" – it can mean deities in general or be the name for a particular God. Biblical scholars gave names to the suspected origin of the gods in the Torah – E to a writer from the north of Canaan where the God El was venerated, and J to one from the South, from Judea where a god named Yahweh existed next to the old Caananite god Baal, the storm god. For a while, Yahweh had a consort by the name of Asherah, just like El. There are earlier Egyptian references to a "Yhw" which seemed to have been not a god but a place, situated somewhere in Edom in the south of Judea, "the land of the Shasu". For a time it seems that El from the North and Yahweh from the South merged somewhat (El the god of compassion, and Yahweh the god of war), both lending their characteristics to the other over time.

Child sacrifice in times of great peril was an accepted rite in many Middle Eastern countries, including Egypt and also Canaan. Prof. Mark S. Smith in his book "The Early History of God" quotes verses from various books in the Bible showing that child-sacrifice was also practiced by adherents of the Yahweh cult, even down to the 7th century BCE, showing its Canaanite roots.

In 922 BCE, the Assyrians conquered Samaria, the northern part of the country. From then on the worship of El as god of the conquered people slowly gave way to veneration of Yahweh, who was anchored in

Judea and eventually gave up Asherah as his consort. In 586 BCE Babylon conquered Judea and deported Jews to what is now Iraq, where the exiles lived for 50 years before they were allowed back by the Greeks, who took over the entire Middle East and hellenized the country. After the Greeks, the Romans conquered the land and made it a province of Rome.

At this time, writing became the main mode of storing narratives and memories, surpassing the oral transmission mode. In the latter half of the monarchy, it became the preferred way to anchor prophesies and make them available to a wider audience. The idea arose that Yahweh was not just one of a circle of gods, or even the god of the state, but rather the only true deity in the cosmos.

The oldest surviving text from the Hebrew Bible, dating from around 600 BCE, is on two silver amulets found in 1979 in a burial cave southwest of the Old City of Jerusalem. They are inscribed in Biblical Hebrew with portions of the Priestly Blessing from the Book of Numbers 6:24-26):

> May the LORD bless you and keep you
>
> May the LORD make His face shine upon you and be gracious to you -
>
> May the LORD lift up His face unto you and give you peace

Here are photos of the front and back of a jewelry reproduction, purchased in Jerusalem, of one of the scrolls.

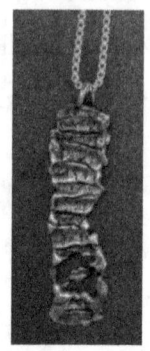 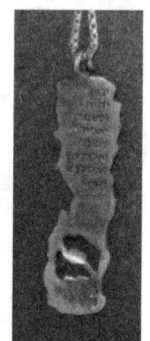

During the exile in Babylon and the time afterwards, priests whose religious direction was anchored in Judea, worked on the compilation of the Torah, creating the Judaic Bible as we know it now. They built the foundation of a consistent Judaism centralizing the acceptance of Yahweh as the monotheistic God of the Jews.

Richard Elliott Friedman did an intensive study in his book *Who Wrote the Bible* and pinpointed the origin of the various Bible stories. They give deep insight into the timeline, change of customs and moral development.

It turns out that Yahweh did not suddenly reveal himself. Nor was he brought to Canaan by Moses from Egypt or by Abraham from Sumer. He evolved over time and through tribes rooted in Canaan. He even incorporated in himself traits and practices of the old Canaanite gods. The efforts of the Torah writers resulted in the formation of a god who was believed to be the one and only God worthy of veneration, transcendent and ethical: the God of the Jews, the God of the Chosen People.

Why did the Israelites succeed where the other tribes failed? There may be many reasons, but one explanation makes sense to me above all others, and it is this:

The Gospel of St. John 1:1 says: "In the beginning was the Word, and the Word was with God, and the Word was God." As a child, sitting through many Sunday services in my Lutheran Church, I could never understand what that meant and nobody was able to explain it to me to my satisfaction. But when I was thinking about the fabulous development of the Jewish people (from a little tribe in Canaan to the diaspora and settlement all over the world, with accomplishments and intelligence and success and moral and ethical developments), I recognized that for them, too, the beginning was the Word. The Word as in language, as in communication, as in oral transmission; as a bond between people, the formation of letters on bone, on stone, on animal hide, on papyrus, and on paper; as in a depository of knowledge and wisdom. There were men who loved to think in words and who communicated them; who had visions, imagination, prophecies; who collected tales from the distant past and worked with others to combine the treasures of a people into a book to enlighten, instruct and guide them, build a culture as well as promote it, build a religion and undergird it with the results of their memories and hopes. Among all

47

the people in Canaan, as far as we know, only the Israelites accomplished that. After a while the Word, as enshrined in the Torah, became a living presence in their lives, enhanced by the Talmud and the Midrash, and made joyous by festivals and commemorations. The Word, after a while, took on a life of its own.

THE CHARACTER OF THE JEWISH PEOPLE

Arthur Hertzberg and Aron Hirt-Manheimer in their book "Jews" speak about the essential Jewish qualities of "the chosen, the factious, and the outsider" and contend that there is a definable Jewish character that has manifested itself in Jews over the centuries. They speak about three basic parts of this personality profile: the self-image of Jews as a chosen people; Jews historically prone to internal dissension and always challenging the majority's beliefs, and Jews as the quintessential outsiders in Western civilization. Out of these three traits I consider chosenness the first and crucial part, determining the development of the other two.

Chosenness: According to the Bible, both Abraham and Moses took part in a covenant between God and the Israelites that proclaimed them as his specially chosen people. This "scandal of particularism" has always been problematic. Why would God choose, when he could have revealed himself to all mankind?

But over the centuries, during the hard times while surrounded by hostile tribes in Palestine and the hard times in the diaspora with its pogroms and anti-Semitism, the knowledge that they were chosen by God above all others became the very core of the Jews' self-image. They took in the unshakeable conviction of being God's choice with their mother's milk – it was bred into their bones. Even secular Jews who do not see their lives in a religious context, still feel in the depth of their being that they are special and under the protection of God (which gives them a certainty and confidence other people don't have). It elevates them in their own minds, and gives them comfort and purpose, even through hardships and misery.

There are two main viewpoints of chosenness. The first group believes that God made them special because He gave them the task of being a "light to the nations": undertaking the moral mission to struggle for universal justice, peace and compassion, being "the self-chosen bearers of a unique, incandescent message" (as Arthur Hertzberg puts it). Herein lies the reason for the countless moral and ethical teachings and guidelines inherent in the Jewish faith which also influenced other religions and situations over time. It is not an easy responsibility: Arthur Hertzberg says that "chosenness is the ever-present, and inescapable, discomfort caused by conscience."

It is also true that some Jewish thinkers have interpreted chosenness to mean that there is a qualitative difference between Jews and other people, and that Jews belong to a different category altogether. Observant Jews thank God every morning that they are not a Gentile or a woman, in the full conviction that they are better than them. The Talmud contains many exhortations of a humanistic, universal nature, but it also expresses the feeling of superiority over gentiles (non-Jews). The right-wing minority in Israel today, basing its belief in the absolute veracity of the Bible, think that power and conquest will be the solution and that they have a right to the land because it was given to them by God 3000 years ago. It must be remembered that their actions are to be counted not against "the Jews", but against a small, indoctrinated and fundamentalist number of them. Many comparisons can be found here: only a small percentage of Germans were Nazis, only a small percentage of American whites were members of the KKK, only a small percentage of Muslims belong to the Taliban, only a small percentage of the Spanish were fascists during the 30's. It is the ultra right-wing of any group that needs to be feared. This has grave consequences for peace in the Middle East, as described in the chapters on Zionism and Fundamentalism.

We know now that the narratives of Abraham and his sons Ishmael and Isaac (around 1995 BCE), Moses and his people's exodus from Egypt (around 1300 BCE), and King David (around 900 BCE) were handed down by oral transmission for hundreds of years before they were collected, rewritten by E, J and P, and edited, added to, and interpreted by priests and rabbis and visionaries and wise men, and woven into a patchwork of stories around the time of the Babylonian exile (about 550 BCE). It is even quite possible, and in the case of the Exodus quite certain, that the origin of the narratives was never based on fact, but was influenced by the desire of the sages of ancient times to give encouragement and confidence and the pride of history to the Israelites - and the certainty of a future. Archaeological discoveries are therefore now simply disregarded by those who do not waiver in their belief that the Bible represents the eternal truth of their heritage. Many Jews cannot face the acknowledgement that the Bible may not be the full truth, because it would put their entire belief, faith, history, culture, identity and future into question.

Keeping this in mind, it must be said that, psychologically, it was a brilliant stroke of genius to declare the Israelite people God's chosen. Nothing had more influence on the Jews over the centuries than this. From a wider philosophical view, though, it must also be recognized that the mind of a human is too small to encompass all aspects of the entire truth. We have to accept one explanation because we need to build our lives around what looks like the truth to us, but we also need to examine the world and hold ourselves in abeyance to find out whether another explanation is closer to the truth. In the Middle Ages in Europe, people were executed by Christian authorities because they did not believe that the earth was the center of the universe (until more was known and our eyes saw other irregularities and created more doubt).

Perhaps, in a global, more crowded world, the tribal particularism of the past needs to be replaced with large-scale universalism. That basic human concern should be the inherent worth of all individuals of any religious, national, racial and ethnic origin, instead of the welfare and interest of a selected part of one particular group. The question: "Is it good or bad for the Jews?" in evaluating any problem should now be "Is it good or bad for Mankind?"

Factiousness: It is said, as a joke, that if there are two Jews in a discussion, there are three opinions. Jews have been historically prone to internal dissensions and resistant to majority opinion in their social group. The knowledge of one's chosenness by God plays a role in one's self-confidence, one's creativity, one's courage to diverge and to dare, one's courage to gamble. Nothing can go wrong if God is with you, and it doesn't really matter whether He is or is not – what counts is your perception. The truth is not out there all by itself, like the Rock of Gibraltar, but in your mind like a picture chiseled in stone.

Being among the chosen necessitates a community of the chosen. In addition, the hostility of those not chosen encouraged Jews to seek comfortable environments of shared faith, religion, customs, history. Despite the factiousness, there is tremendous cohesion among Jews. People all over the world have found friends and help wherever they landed in a new country. In their personal and communal lives, they formed a united front, unobtrusive perhaps, but real. However, the divisiveness within, throughout history, was often serious and tragic.

53

Right from the beginning, the Jewish people were divided between those who wanted to remain true to Yahweh and those who wanted to worship pagan idols; who wanted to remain Jews and those who wanted to assimilate into the prevailing culture. In ancient times there were revolutionaries like the Maccabees and the Zealots, groups like the Saducces and the Pharasees. Before Jerusalem was destroyed in 70 CE by the Romans, the factions within the city fought one another viciously, none of them seeking compromise. During the Holocaust American Jews did perhaps not do enough to save those expelled from other countries. Nowadays there are ultra-orthodox, orthodox, conservative and reform branches and a whole array of Hasidic organizations and rabbis with loyal followers. Depending on their country of origin, there are Ashkenazim, Sephardim and Oriental Jews with different histories and narratives. Some helped Jews escape from the Nazi persecution, and others refused to get involved. Jews were also to be found actively working for Communism, Socialism, Trade Unionism and on every spectrum imaginable.

Jesus the Jew was another of those revolutionaries. He was born and raised as a Jew and died as one, but in his life he realized that not just Jews, but all human beings are children of God: the downtrodden, the despairing, the sinful, the foreign. And God's love is on all of them. Furthermore, he saw the strict adherence and obedience to religious laws as meaningless if, in life, there was no effort to translate God's will into good works and action. Jesus, the revolutionary, moved from the idea of exclusivity of the Jews to universality of all mankind. He recognized that following ritual is less important than a life lived in compassion and action. Jesus never wrote a word and the gospels may be quoting words he never said. The first Gospel was written 60 years of his death, and in Christianity also myths, projection, wishful thinking and *purposeful interpretation* evolved into a religion and a theology that, I am sure, he would not recognize today. Both in Christianity and in Judaism, faith, belief, need and desire for certainty prevail and persist despite doubt and rational arguments to the contrary..

Today, in Israel, there are dozens of political parties along the full spectrum, with many fighting each other bitterly. They are divided between those who challenge the leadership and those who want to be united; between those who would be willing to compromise for the sake of peace and those who are willing to make war in the face of any compromise; those who are Zionists standing behind the State of Israel and those, like the orthodox adherents of Neturei Karta, who are orthodox Jews united against Zionism. The National Religious Party and the Ultra-Orthodox represent the far-right, fundamentalist wing extending great influence on Israeli politics and, by extension, on the politics of the United States.

In the midst of these, there is a large number of left-leaning peace organizations working against the Israeli occupation, against house demolitions, for the rights of Palestinians, for a return to a "Jewishness" and the "Jewish soul" that they feel Israel has lost by virtue of the occupation and suppression of the Palestinians.

Despite all of this dissension, Jews, religious and secular, agree that Israel is important to them, whether they live in Israel or decide to stay in some other country. They love Israel, even though they may be critical of its actions. Arthur Herzberg says:

> "Contemporary Israel takes Jews beyond their age-old factionalism to the bedrock of their innermost identity. It assures Jews that they are an eternal people."

Outsider: Wherever he lived during the diaspora years, the Jew often was an outsider. He and his family had to find a place in societies that tolerated him and then suddenly might turn against him. He always had to be prepared to flee, being nowhere at home. Even friends turned against him when trouble arose, and the greatest proof of that was found in Germany, an enlightened country that made room for his Jewishness and then unleashed the genocide called Holocaust upon him.

The world kept Jews at a distance. But the Jews themselves, bolstered by the history of their chosenness, kept themselves apart and separate also. A Greco-Egyptian priest in the third century BCE, called Manetho, complained that the "Jews do not eat and drink with us; they do not participate in our civic life; they marry only other Jews, and they believe that their God is superior to ours". Later Romans, like Cicero and Seneca, also expressed complaints about these traits.

Arthur Herzberg asks in his book:

"Do the Jews make any contribution to anti-Semitism? The answer is, fundamentally and unavoidably, yes. Their contribution to Jew-hatred is that they insist on being Jews; by definition they challenge the dominant dogmas."

Jews have always struggled to maintain a separate and special culture, even as they tried to be accepted by the majority. Did that perhaps contribute to the development of anti-Semitism? I remember from my German nationalistic childhood, anchored in loyalty to the State, a quiet resentment about those who took the best Germany had to offer, yet kept apart and fervently hoped to be "next year in Jerusalem. Many Jews (taking into consideration the factiousness of the Jewish people) do not see themselves primarily as citizens of their home country, but as Jews and as God's chosen people first and foremost. The particularism and separateness is twofold; caused by them, and forced on them as well.

The State of Israel

ISRAEL, JEWISH AND DEMOCRATIC

Israel is a beautiful country, well organized, with all the amenities and modern features of other advanced nations of the world. It is among the first in science and scientific accomplishments, in art, music, film, theater, restaurants, etc., a true homeland for Jews from all over the world. When you land at the airport in Tel Aviv, the sweet smell of orange blossoms and the mild soft breezes envelope you with the promise of enjoyable days to come. I loved Israel with all my heart. I enjoyed its vistas, its freedom, its friendly welcome and the history and exotic features that distinguished it from my country of origin. But what visitors see is not the entire picture.

Zionism is a movement, founded by Theodor Herzl in the 19th century, which aimed to give the persecuted Jews of the world a homeland in

59

the country of their origin. The Holocaust in Europe accelerated this need with the result that, in 1948, the United Nations granted statehood to Israel as a "homeland for the Jews". It was also very clear from the beginning, even though not explicitly stated, that a "homeland for the Jews" was intended to be a Jewish State with full sovereignity and power in Jewish hands and for Jews alone. This development is described in detail and with a pervasive desire for honesty and truth by Michael Neumann in his book *The Case against Israel*.

Zionism was seeking the return of the Jewish people to the land of their origin, using the slogan "A land without people for a people without land". But in 1919 David Ben Gurion wrote:

> "Everybody sees the problem in the relations between the Jews and the [Palestinian] Arabs. But not everybody sees that there's no solution to it. There is no solution! . . . The conflict between the interests of the Jews and the interests of the [Palestinian] Arabs in Palestine cannot be resolved by sophisms. I don't know any Arabs who would agree to Palestine being ours---even if we learn Arabic . . . There's a national question here. We want the country to be ours. The Arabs want the country to be theirs."[5]

This quote shows that, right from the beginning, there was a very clear understanding of the fact that the return of the Jews to Israel would entail the disenfranchisement and expulsion of the Arabs. When the war broke out after the granting of statehood, 700,000 Arab inhabitants left their homes in fear for their lives. Most expected to return soon. And many were killed or driven out by the Jewish militias following the

---

[5] Segev, Tom, One Palestine, Complete, *p. 116*

new policy mandating "transfer" of the existing population. These former occupants of Palestine reside now in refugee camps in surrounding countries as well as the West Bank and Gaza, and in Arab villages in Israel itself. While Israelis celebrate Independence Day, Palestinians remember the Naqba, the Catastrophe when they were ejected from their land and subjected to occupation.

Today 1.6 Million Arabs, representing about 20% of the population, are Israeli citizens in a country of 7,600,000 inhabitants. They have Israeli citizenship but live in crowded and neglected villages, often without paved streets, postal service, house numbers, utility lines, parks, playgrounds and open spaces. More than 400 Arab villages were depopulated and have disappeared from maps. Authorities do not grant building permits to Arabs, and destroy any buildings that have been built without permits. As a result, many people are made homeless. In Arab villages inside Israel, tens of thousands of homes are judged illegal and are under threat of demolition. High walls separate settlements from Arab villages and innumerable military checkpoints hamper free movement of the population. Arab-owned agricultural lands, often in the possession of their families for hundreds of years, were and still are confiscated without any payment and given to Jewish villages for housing and farming - depriving Arab families of income from their property. Thousands of Palestinians are confined in prison in "administrative detention", meaning incarceration without charge or trial, often in solitary confinement. Are we outraged?

Guantanamo holds hundreds of suspected terrorists without trial since 2004.

CIA remote-sensing map, 2008

In June 1967, after an escalation of tensions between Israel and the surrounding Arab states of Egypt, Syria and Jordan, Israel started the Six-Day War by launching surprise bombing raids against Egyptian air-fields and in three days captured the West Bank, Gaza, the Golan Heights and East Jerusalem. Miko Peled, whose father, Matti Peled, was one of the generals in the campaign, relates in his book "The General's Son" that his father had expected a limited war with Egypt to punish the Egyptians for their breach of a ceasefire and to assert Israeli military might. Now he was deeply disturbed by the conquest of the Palestinian land which had never been part of any official plan. At the first meeting of the General Staff after the war, General Peled spoke these fateful words: "For the first time in Israel's history, we are face to face with the Palestinians, without other Arab countries dividing us. Now we have a chance to offer the Palestinians a state of their own."[6] He warned that, if these lands were kept, popular resistance to the occupation was sure to develop. He also foresaw great moral danger to the Jewish state because of the certain need to brutally suppress the Palestinians. Nobody listened to him. In fact, he was told by Yitzhak Rabin that the political climate at that time did not allow these discussions.

With the exception of East Jerusalem where about 2 million Palestinians live, the West Bank was not annexed by Israel but has remained under Israeli military control and is referred to by Israel as Judea and Samaria. It is inhabited by over 2 Million Palestinians and about 350,000 Jews who live in illegal and internationally unrecognized settlements including East Jerusalem. Limited access roads crisscross the West Bank to connect the illegal settlements occupied by Jewish settlers and separate the Palestinians from their land and neighboring villages.

Life in the occupied zone is heartbreakingly difficult. Palestinian villages and homes are mostly poor, cramped and overpopulated, perhaps suitable 50 years ago, but not when needing to house three generations of parents and children. A Palestinian may not build or

---

[6] Miko Peled, *The General's Son"*, pg 48/49

add to a house for his family without permits, and permits are not given. If he does try to build, the soldiers will come and tear the structure down. High walls, ghetto-like, run along the inside of large sections of the border to separate Israel from the Palestinian-occupied areas. Water is pumped to the settlements first, leaving Palestinians only a few hours of water access per day. Going anywhere means standing for hours at checkpoints. Medical care is minimal, and people sometimes die in ambulances because the army won't open the checkpoint to let them through. Palestinian produce has to wait long hours in trucks before it is allowed across the border, and often rots in the fields because soldiers prevent access. The human burden is tremendous: the difficulty to find work to provide for one's family, the hardship of getting to work or school through checkpoints and road closings, the hopelessness and despair underlying every new day, the need to deal with the occupiers' insults, and the constant effort to affirm one's value and self-respect while being treated as a second-class citizen.

Attempts at a peaceful solution have not shown success in 45 years, the main obstacle being the occupied territories and East Jerusalem and the construction of new settlements. It became clear to me that the beautiful society I so much admired when I first came to Israel, violently excluded another people from their land, and was built on the suffering and loss of the indigenous population.

Behind the sweet smell of orange blossom and the mild breezes, the State of Israel, founded on the basis of Zionism, shows that, while it keeps the memory of the Holocaust and Jewish suffering alive, it displays no concern about the expulsion and suppression of the Palestinians nor compassion for them.

THE MYTHS OF ZIONISM

The Declaration of the Establishment of the State of Israel reads:

> After being forcibly exiled from their land, the people kept faith
> with it throughout their Dispersion and never ceased to pray
> and hope for their return to it and for the restoration in it of
> their political freedom.

Prof. John Rose in his "The Myths of Zionism" examines a number of
myths which form the core of Zionism and shaped the creation and
support the continued existence of the State of Israel. The Oxford
Dictionary makes a distinction between a lie which "is an intentionally
false statement", a "deliberate deception", and a myth which is "a
widely held but false notion", without necessarily deceptive intent. As
Ben-Gurion explained:

"It is not important whether the story is a true record of an event or not. What is of importance is that this is what the Jews believed as far back as the period of the First Temple."

However, to people who experience injustice and oppression based on a myth or a falsehood, as Prof. Rose states, it doesn't matter whether the suffering is based on an intentional lie or a false notion.

The Bible as Mandate.

David Ben-Gurion, the main founder and first Prime Minister of the State of Israel, based the right of Jews to the land of Israel on

- The assertion of historical truth in the Bible,

- the biblical promise that God made to his chosen people, and

- the existence of the ancient Israelite kingdom of David (about 1000 to 922 BCE)

This is the point which is discredited by the archaeological discoveries in the last fifty years. The excavations throw doubt on the Exodus and therefore on Moses on Mt. Sinai and the entire structure of the Bible itself (as explained before). The archaeologists excavated Jerusalem again and again and failed to find evidence of any tenth century occupation – no monumental architecture, no pottery remnants. No single trace of any Israelite literary activity during this period was ever discovered. The great kingdom, as described in the Bible, only existed for less than 100 years and is, according to Finkelstein and Silverman, "the figment of some of the ancient world's most creative

68

imaginations". They are certain, based on their discoveries, that Jerusalem was, at King David's time, not more than a small tribal village where pagan gods were still venerated side by side with Yahweh and his consort Asherath.

The Bible was written much later, during the Babylonian exile and the Persian Period. Jeremiah, a prophet during these dark days, writes in Jeremiah VIII: 8: "How can you say: "We are wise, and the law of the LORD is with us". But, behold, the false pen of the scribes has made it into a lie." Was Jeremiah already wondering about the myths being incorporated into the Bible?

The Bible makes one believe that the small land of Canaan was only settled by Israelites who staked their claims there. Instead it was populated at this time not only by them, but also by Canaanite Hittites, Amorites, Perizzites, Hivites, Girgashites, Jebusites, Philistines, Ammonites, Moabites, and Edomites who had their own substantial city-states, their own governments, their own gods, and their own culture.

Rose agrees with Finkelstein and Silberman that the Bible is

> "a sacred scripture of unparalleled literacy and spiritual genius … an epic saga woven together from an astonishingly rich collection of historical writings, memories, legends, folk tales, anecdotes, royal propaganda, prophecy and ancient poetry …"[7]

---

[7] John Rose, The Myths of Zionism, page 25

... but it is not History, and therefore needs to be approached with caution.

Exile – the Distinguishing Characteristics of the Jews. Zionism has built its justification on the fact that since the Roman Exile the Jews have wandered, homeless, through foreign lands and longed for the return to their own homeland.

However, substantial Jewish communities had existed in many parts of the Middle East long before 70 CE, when Rome put down the Jewish Revolt in Judaea and destroyed the Temple at Jerusalem. There were settlements during Babylonian times in Iraq and Iran which had, until the creation of Israel, well-established and thriving communities. The same is true for Elephantine in Egypt. After the victory of Greece in 336 – 323 BCE there was a migration of many Jews into the Greek Empire, following Greek promises of protection and respect. They settled in Alexandria with great success, making up no less than a third of the entire population. When the Roman Empire took over, many settled all around the Mediterranean in Roman-governed areas. By that time *the majority of Jews were living outside Judea.*[8].

Expatriates also did not think of Israel or Judea or Jerusalem as their "homeland". One's home was the city, country, and place of one's

---

[8] John Rose, page 39

education; the actual place and context one was born into. (See also pages 29ff)

Eighteen Centuries of Jewish Suffering. In the Zionist view of history, Jewish communities in the diaspora throughout the Middle East, in Europe, China and finally in America were powerless and impoverished and longed for the return to their homeland. Theodore Herzl argued that only the transfer of Jews to Palestine could end this suffering.

Modern Jewish studies have finally come to realize that, not only was there a thriving merchant class in antiquity, but also a large number of well-to-do traders, government officials, innovators, mediators, linguists and scientists existing continuously to modern times. Jews, far from being on the outer margins of society, were quite often close to the centers of powers because of their banking abilities and connections to ruling houses.

It is true that Jews had to pay a higher tax rate and needed to adjust to prevailing governments, but their economic role and outstanding talent made them invaluable and therefore protected. Their wealth and economic stature even induced other religions and nationals to convert to Judaism.

There were also times of anti-Semitism presenting danger to life and property, like the crusades and Christian inquisition, which culminated

71

to expulsion and, when possible, migration to less dangerous countries. The Holocaust, by far the most horrible persecution of Jews, strengthened the Zionist conviction that a Jewish homeland would grant a haven to Jews forever. But even hard times did not lead to a universal Jewish return to Jerusalem and Palestine. In fact, even after the founding of the Jewish and Democratic State of Israel, many Jews from different countries preferred to go to the United States instead of Israel. Today, even Germany and Poland have rising numbers of Jewish citizens despite their role in the Holocaust.

We must recognize, however, how "intense anti-Jewish feeling is fuelled when Jews deny democracy to others in the land they claim exclusively belongs to them."[9]

'Us' Jews, 'Them' Arabs: Another fundamentalist Zionist myth is that Arabs and Jews are so different (with Arabs inferior) that they cannot live together. It is quite interesting to see how the split among Jews affects their convictions, depending on their area of origin.

The Sephardim, those Jews originally from Spain and then living in Muslim countries of North Africa and the Middle East, as well as the Oriental Jews living for centuries in Iraq and Iran and Palestine itself, are not as passionately involved in the Holocaust, but have in fact an Arabic-Jewish culture through a close relationship with their Arab

---

[9] John Rose, p 62

neighbors. Where they came from, they did not live in separate areas, but in close proximity to one another. Muslims and Jews observed their own religions, but were good neighbors, sharing and borrowing possessions and sometimes jointly owning houses. Their songs, their shared cultural frame of reference, even the use of Arabic was shared by both groups. Sometimes Sephardim actually look more Arab than Jewish and also identify themselves as Arab Jews.

In the late nineteenth century, a locked room was discovered in an eleventh-century Cairo synagogue called Geniza. It contained pieces of paper, contracts, letters etc., untouched for hundreds of years, which gave a look into the close-knit Jewish-Arab communities. The find constitutes a true mirror of life, very wide in scope and reflecting many aspects of the society that existed then.

Ashkenazi Jews, the Israelis from Europe, Poland and Russia, hold the Holocaust as an eternal memory, but consider Arabs as strangers and different. Since Zionism was promoted by Ashkenazi Jews and the State of Israel was founded and is currently governed by them, both Zionism and the State of Israel carry the Ashkenazi viewpoint. The Sephardim or Mizrahim, Arabized for centuries, abruptly dislodged from their cultural homes, brought "home" to Israel, and forced to assume a homogeneous European identity, were subjected by this devastating dislocation to "a profound and visceral schizophrenia". Prof. Ella Habiba Shohat, in her essay *"The Mizrahim in Israel. - Zionism from the perspective of its Jewish victims"* gives deep insight into the souls of Israeli citizens who identify as and with Arabs.

73

A Land Without People…...

The Zionists called Palestine a neglected and poor country, run down and undeveloped, and labeled the Arabs occupying that land as unable or unwilling to expend the effort to improve and beautify it. They proclaimed that it was the Jews who "made the desert bloom", who converted the neglected country into a showcase. In reality, Palestine before Israel, was a densely settled agrarian society with thousands of prosperous villages and a thriving trade in olive oil, pottery, soap etc. Nablus is an example of a beautiful town, with close connections to a number of villages with flourishing social and private relationships, that gave stability and structure to the society. Palestine was definitely not an empty land and not a neglected one. Asher Ginsberg visited Palestine in 1891 and wrote[10]:

> "We abroad have a way of thinking that Palestine today is almost desert, an uncultivated wilderness, and that anyone who wishes to buy land there can do so to his heart's content. But this is not in fact the case. It is difficult to find any uncultivated land anywhere in the country …"

Herbert Samuel, British High Commissioner for Palestine, wrote in a personal letter to Weizman in 1921[11]:

---

[10] Ginsberg, Asher, quoted in *The Decadence of Judaism in our Time, Institute of Palestinian Studies, Beirut, 1969*

[11] Samuel, Herbert, as quoted in John H. Davis *The Evasive Peace*, pp. 61

"After a year in Palestine I have come to the conclusion that the importance of the Arab factor had been underestimated by the Zionist movement: unless there is very careful steering it is upon the Arab rock that the Zionist ship may be wrecked."

Moshe Sharett[12] warned in 1936:

"There is no Arab in Palestine who is not harmed by Jewish immigration; there is no Arab who does not feel himself part of the Great Arab Nation ... For him Palestine is an independent unit that had an Arab face ...."

It is obvious that the reason for today's conflict was the settlement of one people on the land of another. David Ben-Gurion showed that he understood the situation very well. He stated in a speech before the Mapai Political Committee in 1938[13]:

"This is an active resistance by the Palestinians to what they regard as an usurpation of their homeland by the Jews – that's why they fight .... In our political argument abroad, we minimize Arab opposition to us. But let us not ignore the truth among ourselves. I insist on the truth, not out of respect for scientific but political realities. The acknowledgment of this truth leads to inevitable and serious conclusions regarding our work in Palestine ... the fighting is only one aspect of the conflict which is in essence a political one. And politically we are the aggressors and they defend themselves. Militarily, it is we who are on the defensive, who have the upper hand ... but in the political sphere they are superior. ... The country is theirs, because they inhabit it, whereas we want to come here and settle down, and in their view we want to take away from them their country, while we are still outside."

---

[12] Sharett, Moshe, quoted in John H. Davis *The Evasive Peace, pp. 14-15,46*

[13] Ben-Gurion, David, *The History of the Haganah*, World Zionist Organization, 1954, pages 141-142

While decent men communicated their unease and their doubts, the Zionist leaders wiped away these doubts and hesitancy by affirming their right to the land by aggression, consistent with Machiavelli's "The end justifies the means". Ben-Gurion summed up the goals of the Zionist movement in the introduction to The History of the Haganah[14]:

> "At the present time we speak of colonization, and only of colonization. It is our short-term objective. But it is clear that England belongs to the English, Egypt to the Egyptians and Judea to the Jews. In our country there is room only for Jews. We will say to the Arabs: 'Move over'; if they are not in agreement, if they resist, we will push them by force."

Joseph Weitz, a Jewish government official, wrote in 1940[15]:

> "It must be clear that there is no room for both peoples in this country …. There is no room for compromise on this point! The Zionist enterprise so far, in terms of preparing the ground and paving the way for the creation of the Hebrew State in the land of Israel, has been fine and good in its own time, and could do with 'land-buying' – but this will not bring about the State of Israel; … and there is no way besides transferring the Arabs from here to neighboring countries, to transfer all of them, not one village, not one tribe should be left. And only with such a transfer will the country be able to absorb millions of our brothers, and the Jewish questions shall be solved, once and for all. There is no other way out."

And finally Menachem Begin[16]

---

[14] Ben-Gurion, David, ibid

[15] Weitz, Joseph, *My Diary and Letters to the Children,* Tel Aviv, 1940

[16] Begin, Menachem, The History of the Haganah, *World Zionist Organization,* 1954

"In our country there is only room for Jews".

The above quotes show that the early leaders like Theodore Herzl and Chaim Weisman worked for the creation of a Jewish homeland in Palestine, but always intended this homeland to be in the form of a Jewish state. As the number of settlers increased, it became inevitable that a backlash movement would develop among the Arabs who feared losing control of their country. It was therefore not possible – and it could never have been possible – to pursue colonization and settlement by peaceful means. The aims of the Jewish leadership were so incompatible with those of the Arabs, that conflict and friction became inevitable. The Palestinians used violence to protect their interests against a growing immigrant population, and the Jews, in turn, used violence to establish themselves in a hostile environment.

Nations and organizations very often plan broad-based strategies without concern and consideration for the common man and the situation on the ground. In this case the victims of the Holocaust became the collective oppressors of others. In such a world of conflict between victims and executioners, it is the job of thinking people, as Albert Camus said, not to be on the side of the executioners.

Observing human nature, human beings focus on "the other" or are compelled to create the concept of "the other", to justify actions they consider important for their own survival and advancement. The Jews, Germany's "others", so cruelly persecuted and mistreated, cannot be blamed for wanting their own space. It is not a crime to want to preserve one's own identity. It is, however, a crime when others are dehumanized in the process – denied basic human rights. If we want peace on this crowded planet, the paradigm of competition must be replaced by that of cooperation. Palestinians, in the attempt to do their share for peace, initially gave up 78% of their land, a painful concession which puts all those to shame who believe the Israeli accusation that Palestinians are unwilling to compromise and be a "partner for peace".

I wonder what the situation would look like today if Zionism had originally been founded as a State for Jews and Arabs, as my Kibbutz friend Dov had hoped. That did not happen, and instead we find two wounded, determined parties now facing "the other". Each side is claiming the same strip of land and denying the other's right to it. Meron Benvenisti[17], the Israeli demographer, describes the conflict as a

> "tribal war, the descendants of Isaac and Ishmael battling over land with stones and clubs."

And finally the voice of Abba Eban, one of Israel's wisest statesmen and its most passionate defender:

> "If we insist on ruling an entire territory and population (which was never envisioned when we made the dramatic breakthrough to Jewish statehood), we shall soon lose our Jewish majority, our democratic principles, our hope of ultimate peace, the prospect of avoiding war, the maintenance of our international friendships, the durability of the Egyptian treaty relationship and any chance of a national consensus at

---

[17] Benvenisti, Meron, *West Bank Enmity Takes on The Marks of Permanence*, New York Times, February 21, 1988, E-2

home. The status quo is the least viable and the most catastrophic of all the Israeli options."[18]

... for a People without Land

By the end of the 19th century the majority of a world population of almost eight million Jews lived in Eastern Europe, four million of them in the "Pale of Settlement", the area between Poland and the Ukraine, reaching up to Lithuania and down to the Caucasus which was the concentrated area of settlement for Jews. Prof. John Rose gives a detailed description of the intricate political events around the turn of the century. In this small book only the main ideas could be mentioned.

The pogroms during the last part of the 19th century had a number of results. Namely, the movement of Jews from the small Jewish towns into larger towns and into employment as craftsmen in the general population, and an increasing radicalization leading to organizations built on socialism, trade-unionism and communism with the aim to change the political and human rights situation in Russia, Poland and the Ukraine. Jews were active in all of them. The ideas of the French Revolution were in the air and fostered the hope that the enlightenment of Western Europe could be accomplished in Eastern Europe as well.

---

[18] From an Op-Ed by Abba Eban (former Israel foreign minister and ambassador to The UN and the USA) in the New York Times of Feb. 24, 1988

Mass organizations were formed.   Two Jewish organizations with different aims developed and were working against each other.   They were

- Zionism (promoted by, among others, Herzl, Ben-Gurion and Weitzman) which saw the answer to the Jewish problem in a homeland in Palestine, and

- The Socialist Bund attempting to change the situation on the ground and give the people rights and prospects in the land of their birth.   Self-emancipation, Jewish equal rights and resistance to all forms of anti-Semitism were made an integral part of the revolutionary agenda of the Bund.

Political maneuvering by Herzl and the abuses of anti-Semitism considered unchangeable in the Western world resulted in the Zionist promise that all would be well if people would follow them "to Palestine to build a modern nation in our ancient homeland" (without mentioning that Arabs already lived there).   Herzl also admitted openly, to the horror of his compatriots, that he was ready to "understand and pardon anti-Semitism".   This allowed him to develop a diplomatic agenda in Russia, thereby taking the wind out of the sails of the Bund and of Jewish rights in a newly ordered Russia.

The three possible routes of emancipation facing the Jews in Russia and Poland were:

- Emigration to America
- Emigration to Palestine, or
- Emancipation through struggle to overthrow the current regime.

The Russian Revolution prevented the third solution.

Looking at this development in a European and global perspective, I recognize how interrelated the world's histories are, and how Germany's – and possibly the Jewish people's fate - was influenced by what happened in Russia. In Germany, the lost First World War with its following severe famine, reparation payments, territorial loss, poverty and inflation, was followed in 1919 by the democratic government of the Weimar Republic which unfortunately collapsed. Two main political forces were aligned against each other, their adherents fighting in the streets, namely the internationally oriented Communists with their base in Russia, and the nationally focused National Socialists under an initially obscure Austrian by the name of Adolf Hitler. In the election of 1933, this devastated country was faced with a choice between two evils, and Germany chose that of the nationalist Nazis over the international ideology of Communism.

Immediately after taking power, Hitler issued a Decree nullifying many of the key civil liberties of German citizens. This was widely used as the legal basis for imprisonment of anyone considered to be an opponent of the Nazis, and to suppress publications not considered "friendly" to the Nazi cause. The first inmates in the newly-built concentration camps were actually communists. Today, historians see this decree as the main step in the establishment of a one-party Nazi state in Germany. Creeping loss of civil liberties should signal a strong need for popular engagement, lest we see what happened in Germany overtake democratic rights elsewhere today.

We don't know what would have happened if Germany had turned communist – would there have been a Holocaust and the persecution of the Jews and others? Would there even be a State of Israel now?

When the Soviet Union disintegrated in the 1980's, a massive exodus of over a million Soviet Jews ensued, coming to America in overwhelming numbers. Prime Minister Itzak Shamir intervened and asked President Reagan for help to redirect these Jewish emigrants to Israel, promising to be America's friend in the Middle East – and the rest is history.

FROM POGROMS TO THE HOLOCAUST

According to Prof. Israel Shahak[19], the main difference between a pogrom and the Holocaust is, that the Holocaust was inspired, organized and executed from above, whereas a pogrom was a popular movement which was part of a peasant rebellion of terribly oppressed serfs who were rising against their masters, the clergy and the Jews who happened to be employed as the nobility's tax collectors, estate supervisors and bailiffs and therefore were the "face" of oppression for the oppressed. Jews were not persecuted because of their religion, but because of their socio-economic function as the representatives of the oppressing ruling classes. It is also important to know that in all the worst anti-Jewish persecutions, the king, the aristocracy, the rich and the higher clergy were generally on the side of the Jews, because the activities of the Jews were of benefit to them. Even in Russia pogroms were not tolerated by the Tsarist regime, but could also not

---

[19] Jewish History, Jewish Religion, pgs. 78-79

always be prevented. Rebellions arose when the states themselves were especially weak. All of this does of course not take away the terrible insecurity, the danger and the hardships of the Jews in medieval Europe.

Another kind of crime was the Jew-upon-Jew kind which Prof. Shahak calls a "riot" which was similar in extent to a pogrom. When the governments of Russia, Prussia and Austria became stronger, they deprived the Jewish formerly autonomous communities of the rabbis' power to apply the religious laws and punish heretics. The ordinary criminal law of the countries was now in effect. Those heretics who started to question Judaism and worked towards a more enlightened viewpoint, could now not be openly punished anymore, but the Jewish authorities continued to punish through so-called riots. Prof. Shahak states that "until 1881 in Russia the number of riots by Jews against other Jews probably exceeded the number of pogroms by non-Jews against Jews[20]".

Zionism used the pogroms in the formulation of its aims as a reason for the need to establish a Jewish homeland, and in later years it was the Holocaust itself which reaffirmed this need.

The Holocaust convinced the world of the urgency to establish a Jewish State that would solve the problem of Jewish homelessness by gathering all Jews into their own homeland. The Holocaust is accepted at its core as an event affecting only Jews, even though millions of

---

[20] Jewish Fundamentalism in Israel, pg. 133

other people were its victims, too: gypsies, gays, the disabled, millions of Slavs and other nationalities, Soviet prisoners of war and political dissidents including socialists, communists and priests. Furthermore, the establishment of the Jewish State on "Jewish land" caused the uprooting of the Palestinians, the seizure of their lands, and the death and impoverishment of many.

It is difficult to deal with the events of the Holocaust and its immense pain, sorrow and human tragedy without wanting to make sure that this not ever happen again to Jews, or to people of any other religious, racial, ethnic or national origin. And with that we move from the **particular to the universal**: from the particular Jewish event to similar geopolitical events in the past.

Ian Kershaw, Hitler's biographer, brought two key components of Hitler's worldview together: annihilation of Jewish Bolshevism and new living space (Lebensraum) for Germany. In other words: Jews had to die so Germany could gain new Lebensraum. Genocide is a tool of imperialism in its attempt to establish itself. Victims were not eliminated for what they did, but simply because they existed and were in the way.

Where did this happen before? European colonists virtually wiped out Native Americans because they lived on land coveted by the European settlers. Aborigines were systematically eliminated in Australia. Turkey marched Armenians into the desert and left them to die. The desire for "Lebensraum", as well as the desire to preserve one's own people, prompts the killing of one group so the other group can live. The second atom bomb was dropped at Hiroshima not because it was necessary, but because it saved American lives.

What about Zionism and the Jewish State of Israel, Prof. Rose asks. Should the **particular** needs of the Jews have preference over the ethical need for **a universal** response to the Palestinians? In 1948 750,000 Palestinian Arabs were driven from their land. Many were killed, hundreds of villages were leveled – all so that land could be taken for illegal Jewish settlements. Peace talks begin and end and nothing changes, because Israel "needs" that land. Until now Israel defended the occupation of the territories by focusing on history and security: its right to inherit the land and is obligated to defend it. More recently a third justification was added: Israel needs the land for the "Lebensraum" for Jews.

The Palestinian Delegate-General in the UK, Afif Safieh, wrote the following letter in April, 2001[21];

> ...The Israeli political establishment inflicted on Palestinians four types of denial. First came the denial of our very existence. Then followed the denial of our rights. All this was accompanied by the denial of our sufferings and the denial of their moral and historical responsibility for this suffering. ...
>
> I have never "likened" the Naqba to the Holocaust. My conviction has always been that there is no need for comparisons and historical analogies.

---

[21] Printed with permission of Plutobooks from "The Myth of Zionism" by John Rose.

No one people has a monopoly on human suffering and every ethnic tragedy stands on its own. If I were a Jew or a Gypsy, Nazi barbarity would be the most atrocious event in history. If I were a Black African, it would be slavery and apartheid. If I were a native American, it would be the discovery of the New World by European explorers and settlers that resulted in near-total extermination. If I were an Armenian, it would be the Ottoman massacres. I happen to be a Palestinian, and for me it is the Naqba. Humanity should consider all the above repugnant. I do not consider it advisable to debate hierarchies of suffering. I do not know how to quantify pain or measure suffering. I do know that we are not children of a lesser God".

Insights and Warnings from the Holocaust and the Naqba (reprinted by permission of Plutobooks from "The Myth of Zionism" by John Rose):

"This chapter has tried to challenge the way the Israeli State has used the Holocaust for its own political legitimation. It has been suggested that the *Insights and Warnings* that issue from exploring the tensions between *universal and particular* aspects of the Holocaust point in a very different direction. In a sense these *insights and warnings* are well understood. They coincide with, and have contributed to, what is now a well-founded universalist or international discourse on justice, human rights and citizens' rights, with its unconditional objection to colonial occupation, racism in all its forms, and its defence of the universal rights of refugees. In a very real sense a new international morality is being coded. This underpins the hostile response of international public opinion to the way contemporary Israeli governments conceive of their narrowly defined particularistic needs in the face of the needs of the Palestinian people".

Peter Novick[22] has left us with a final insight on the use of memory about deep grievances. He cites a passage from a son of a Holocaust survivor, a writer called Leon Wieseltier, who warns that the collective memory of oppression can instill

> "..an insolating sense of apartness. It transforms experiences into traditions. Because it abolishes time and dissolves place, collective memory leaves the individual and the group too skeptical about change, does not ready them for discontinuity. … In the memory of oppression, oppression outlives itself. The scar does the work of the wound – injustice retains the power to distort long after it has ceased to be real. It is a posthumous victory for the oppressor, when pain becomes a tradition."

[22] Novick, P., *The Holocaust and Collective Memory* , pg 281

FUNDAMENTALISM

In my study of the impact of Jewish religion on the politics of Israel, I came full circle in my search for the underlying assumptions of Germany's attempted extermination of the Jews (which was my own personal burden of despair) and the hard-line treatment of the Palestinians by the children of the Holocaust in Israel. On a larger scale the question arose: what is the role of fundamentalism in religious doctrines and national ideologies? What is its origin? This small book cannot do justice to the enormous volume of intricate details dealing with the centuries of introspection, debate and commentary.

Profs. Israel Shahak and Norton Mezvinsky wrote the book *Jewish Fundamentalism in Israel* in which they expressed their fear that Jewish fundamentalism in Israel is a major obstacle to peace in the region. They stated further::

> "This book is a journey of understanding—often painful, often dreary, often disturbing—for us as Jews who have a stake in Jewry . With our hearts and minds we want Jews, together with other people, to recognize and strive for the highest ideals, even as we fall short of them. We see these ideals as central to

the values of Western civilization and applicable throughout the civilized world. We believe these values do not stand in the way of peace anywhere. That a perversion of these values in the name of Jewish fundamentalism stands as an impediment to peace, to the development of Israeli democracy and even to civilized discourse outrages us, both as Jews and as human beings".

Fundamentalism is defined as a movement or attitude stressing strict and literal adherence to a set of basic principles and dictates. In Judaism it is an attempt to go back to a context which existed in Jewish communities before the advent of modernity. This objective is the same in Judaism, Christianity and Islam, namely, the restoration and re-establishment of the "original pure faith" which is believed to have existed in the past.

25-30% of Israelis consider themselves secular and comprise those who are influenced by Western ideas of Human Rights, Reason and Activism; 50-55 % are traditional with differing degrees of religious attachment, while about 20% are religiously fundamentalist. This makes about 70% of the population subject to varying degrees of religious indoctrination. Religious Jews in Israel are again divided into two groups. The religiously extreme Haredim arose out of Hasidic communities in Eastern Europe who opposed the Jewish enlightenment during the 19th century. Their followers did not want to submit to the strict authority of the Rabbis and introduced innovations into Jewish worship and life. They wear black wool coats and hats and provide a large percentage of the talmudic students. Religious-national Jews are somewhat more modern and mostly wearing knitted skullcaps.

They form a large part of the settler communities and furiously defend "their right" to the Land of Israel. They also have an extraordinary influence on Israeli politics because the Israeli election laws require the building of coalitions. Religious groups, when asked to join a coalition, demand accommodation to their demands in many areas of public life. Both the Likud and Labor parties kowtow to the religious interests.

The Torah relates that God gave to Abraham and his descendents the land "from the river of Egypt to the great river, the River Euphrates". In their insistence on their right to the land promised by God, the Zionists very prudently refrain from claiming those portions which are now owned by Egypt, Lebanon, Syria, Jordan and Iraq.

Jewish fundamentalists in Israel belong to a wide array of groups with at times differing perspectives and issues. In addition to the sentiments of the exclusiveness of Jews and Israel's separation from other nations, it is important to note that for the Orthodox Jews, the Torah itself is not important unless it is interpreted by Talmudic literature. The Talmud, written over 1,500 years ago in ancient Hebrew and Aramaic, compiles the discussions of some seven or eight generations of scholars. The extensive studies, which Jewish men undertake at Yeshivas, are of the Babylonian Talmud and only secondarily of the Torah, excluding also almost all complete modern subjects like science, philosophy, languages, literature, art, etc. Muslim fundamentalists are similarly educated in Madrassas, focusing entirely on their religion and excluding all other subjects.

Members of the politically religious right insist on Jewish uniqueness – an outgrowth out of the chosenness principle. They also hate the concept of "normality", the idea that Jews are like other people and want to live like other nations. Their perspectives are extreme, without any inclination to consider reason, facts, human compassion, universal rights and values, etc. In that respect they are like most religious Jews, only more so. They are absolutely convinced, as stated in their Talmudic commentaries, of the exclusiveness and superiority of Jews and their separation from other nations because of the values which are important to them.

The Talmud was compiled by several generations of rabbis in the first 500 years of the Common Era. It is not a prescriptive book on ethics, but contains many discussions of an ethical, moral and compassionate nature, but also many others which deal with practical solutions to everyday problems. Some of them stress the exceptional nature of Jews and their religious rights vis-à-vis gentiles, i.e. non-Jews. The problem in this is that some people, misguided or unenlightened, build their understanding of the world on the discussion points that do not stress the dignity of all humans, but rather the superiority of Jews compared with non-Jews.

The Talmud was compiled between 50 and 500 CE at a time when attempts had to be made to bolster Jewish self-image and self-respect, but the sections on Gentiles can still be read and are being studied in synagogues and yeshivas. They result in a certain resentment against

Jews that bubble up in situation of danger, and especially create feelings of hate and anti-semitism.

According to Israel Shahak, neither Zionism nor Israeli politics "could be understood unless the deeper influence of those laws, *and the worldview which they both create and express* is taken into account".[23] Here are some examples from Mr. Shahak's book[24] (not direct quotes):

- Jewish life has an infinite value. There is something more holy and unique about Jewish life than about non-Jewish life. The entire creation of non-Jews exists only for the sake of the Jews. The body of a Jewish person is of a totally different quality from the body of members of all nations of the world.
- Jews killing non-Jews does not constitute murder. Killing of innocent Arabs for reasons of revenge is a Jewish virtue. A Jewish doctor must not treat a Gentile patient or help a Gentile woman give birth.
- It is a grave sin to practice any kind of deception whatsoever against a Jew. Against a Gentile indirect deception is allowed.
- Any prohibition against a deed perpetrated on a Gentile can be waived if it leads to danger that hostility might harm the Jews.
- The hatred for Western culture with its rational and democratic elements is common in the fundamentalist movements of Judaism and Islam.

Rabbi Abraham Kook (1865 - 1935), Israel's first chief rabbi, helped create the settler movement. He preached Jewish supremacy, saying:

---

[23] Shahak, Israel, *Jewish History Jewish Religion, pg. 2,* www.plutopress.com

[24] Shahak, Israel, *Jewish History Jewish Religion*, Chapters 2 and 3

93

"The difference between a Jewish soul and souls of non-Jews - all of them in all different levels - is greater and deeper than the difference between a human soul and the souls of cattle"

and

"non-Jews living under Jewish law in Eretz Ysrael (the Land of Israel) must either be enslaved as water carriers and wood hewers, or banished, or exterminated."

The balance of power defines how Gentiles are to be treated, according to the Halakhah. If the Jews are weak politically, they are advised to do whatever is necessary to prevent hostility and danger to Jews. If they are in power, however, as the Jews are in the State of Israel, then it is their duty to act according to the Talmud, expel the Palestinians, for instance. Mercy only refers to mercy towards Jews.

These laws, at the very least, create an attitude of indifference, scorn or hatred towards Gentiles and certainly influence the attitude towards Palestinians. It must also be kept in mind what the correct meaning is of terms like "fellow", "friend", "man", "neighbor" – they refer to a Jew. Therefore, the saying "thou shalt love thy neighbor like yourself" really is an exhortation to love Jews..

Even though Fundamentalists make up only 20% of the population, it is apparent that hard-line State policies do find support. As Israel Shahak states: "Anyone who lives in Israel knows how deep and widespread these attitudes of hatred and cruelty towards all Gentiles are among a large number of Israeli Jews." Read the story of Baruch Goldstein:

Baruch Goldstein, a follower of Rabbi Meir Kahane, was born in Brooklyn and educated in a Yeshivah and Medical School. He refused, as an army doctor in Israel, to treat Arabs, even if they were Israeli citizens, saying "I am not willing to treat any non-Jew." At his own request he was transferred to Kiryat Arba, where he continued to refuse to treat Arabs and demanded that another army physician be called to substitute for him. His refusal to treat non-Jews was well known to the army command, but he was not disciplined for disobeying commands, even though he had become notorious as an anti-Arab extremist. This reveals the influence of religious parties even in the Israeli army.

In February 1994, Goldstein, in full battle uniform, entered the Muslim prayer hall at the Patriarchs' Cave in Hebron and shot Muslim worshippers kneeling in prayer (mostly in the back), killing 29, including children, and wounding hundreds. Surviving Muslims overpowered and beat him to death.

While Goldstein represented Jewish fundamentalism at its extreme, the government immediately found excuses for this massacre by explaining that Goldstein had been under mental pressure by virtue of having to attend to so many wounded and dead persons, including Arabs. The newspaper articles avoided mentioning the terms "murder", "massacre" or "killing" and used instead "deed", "event" or "occurrence. The unspoken explanation is that according to Halakhic Law the killing of a non-Jew by a Jew is not considered murder.

Within two days of the massacre, posters extolling Goldstein's virtues and complaining that he failed to kill more Arabs, covered the walls of religious neighborhoods. Children of religious settlers came to Jerusalem with buttons reading "Dr. Goldstein cured Israel's ills." Big celebrations were arranged in Goldstein's memory, without protest from any major politician. Goldstein was given an elaborate funeral with the assistance of the highest levels of the Israeli government. A long funeral cortege wound its way through Jerusalem, with the police closing several busy streets in Goldstein's honor. His tomb has become a pilgrimage site for the religious settlers, as well as delegations of religious Jews.

One year after the funeral, the Town of Kiryat Arba obtained a permit to build a large and magnificent memorial on Goldstein's tomb, which has now become a place of pilgrimage. Thousands of Jews come every year from towns in Israel, but also from the United States and France to light candles and pray for "the holy saint and martyr". Goldstein was called a hero, a righteous person, a holy martyr. Rabbis lauded his action as an example for other Jews to follow. Goldstein's actions reinforced the conviction that Jews have a right and duty to kill Gentiles who live in the Land of Israel.

Some of the material in this chapter is from Profs. Israel Shahak and Norton Mezvinsky's book *Jewish Fundamentalism in Israel,* and here is the authors' statement at the end of this chapter:

"Those people, especially Germans, who were silent and did not condemn Nazi ideology before Hitler came to power are also, at least in a moral sense, guilty for the terrible consequences that followed. Similarly, those who are silent and do not condemn Jewish Nazism, as exemplified by the ideologies of Goldstein [and ...], especially if they are Jews, are guilty of the terrible consequences that may yet develop as a result of their silence."

Prof. Shahak, who died in 2001, was a supremely ethical man and a tireless human rights activist. He believed that a merciless self-critique had to go hand-in-hand with a fight for human rights.

Voices for Change

There is nothing one can do about the past. Clans, tribes and nations arose, conquered others and merged. They developed the idea of a God and gave Him omnipotence and laws, consolidated their own character and laid down their own narratives in word and deed. All a writer can do is trace the sparse signs as relics remaining from life and progress, while seeking understanding and compassion in the interpretation of recognized connections and prior interpretations.

Dealing with the topic of Fundamentalism was difficult and reminiscent of Nazi's race hatred against Jews and others and the resulting cruelty and disregard of those others' humanity. These actions created the burden of guilt and shame which I have been carrying all my adult life and gave birth and expression to my hope that people will learn, see and comprehend that neither religion, nor race, nor nationality, nor ethnicity, nothing justifies man's inhumanity to man.

Signs of change are everywhere. Every day newspapers have articles which signal a change in patience, in courage, in resolutions to counter Israel's overwhelming military and political power in the US. The European Union joined the boycott of goods which are manufactured in the West Bank and sold as an Israeli product. It is obvious that the tide is turning by just watching the new openness regarding the policies of the State of Israel and the political aims of the Palestinians.

I am speaking up to express the need for hope: to help bring about future possibilities, to provide clarity of purpose and deeper understanding, to present the insights of courageous and fearless people, to contribute to peace in the Middle East. It is intimidating as every plan for the future is open to attack by different viewpoints, and every plan may fail for any number of reasons. I hope that those with a desire to help heal a fractured world, will work to promote justice and inclusion for all human beings and through this book will find some guidance for the journey forward.

The Talmud also says: "Whosoever preserves a single soul, scripture ascribes [merit] to him as though he had preserved a complete world."

STANDING AGAINST OPPRESSION – RABBI BRANT ROSEN

Rabbi Brant Rosen, born and raised in the United States, is the co-founder and co-chair of the Jewish Voice for Peace Rabbinical Council and has served on the board of Rabbis for Human Rights-North America. He is dedicated to his faith and has identified with Israel deeply all his life. As he explains in his book *Wrestling in the Daylight*, his Jewish identity has been profoundly influenced by the Zionist narrative. He considered himself, however, a "liberal Zionist" and, while disturbed by bad or unjust Israeli policies, he saw them as temporary blemishes on a stable democracy and a noble national project until Israel invaded Lebanon in 1982, attacking with overwhelming military power and causing great destruction and loss to the civilian population. At that time he was less concerned about the safety of Palestinians, but was deeply troubled by the tribal notion that the war was going to "corrupt Israel's soul", as if Jewish life was more important than Palestinian life.. He still suffered in silence, "wrestling in the night", struggling between his faithfulness to Israel and his horror at the inhumane treatment of others.

As a rabbi leading a congregation in the United States, he had been under great pressure to maintain unwavering support for the State of Israel and to keep any criticism in check. But his call to stand up came during Operation Cast Lead, the Israeli assault on Gaza in 2008 when he saw Israel's oppressive treatment of Palestinians. Although he knew that speaking out might have very real professional consequences, speaking out he did. As he said, he was tired of "trying to excuse the inexcusable." He knew without doubt that "my primary religious motivation comes from my inherited Jewish tradition, in which God commands me to stand with the oppressed and to call out the oppressor ... Whenever we diminish the humanity of another, we tarnish the image of God in our world". He is determined to always be motivated by Jewish conscience. It pains him that the State of Israel, born under persecution, has itself become a persecutor and he says that he understands the reason behind Palestinian resistance.

After the Gaza attack, he and several other Rabbis were in contact with Judge Richard Goldstone, who investigated on behalf of the UN Human Rights Commission and issued a 574 page report that blamed BOTH Israel and Hamas for human rights violations. The report caused a "titanic uproar in Israel and throughout the American Jewish communal establishment[25]" for criticizing Israel and subjected Judge Goldstone and his family to intense personal attacks. Judge Goldstone, under Jewish pressure, amended the report somewhat, and the US

---

[25]*Wrestling in the Daylight*, Pg 107

House of Representatives, most certainly also under pressure, passed Resolution 867 by a margin of 344 to 36, that called upon

> "the President and the Secretary of State to oppose unequivocally any endorsement or further consideration of the "Report of the United Nations Fact Finding Mission on the Gaza Conflict" in multilateral fora[26]."

While Israel and the Jewish establishment silenced Judge Goldstone and the US House of Representatives, they did not silence Rabbi Rosen. In different publications and his blog "Rav Shalom" he reveals the change of his thinking and his transformation, and he "wrestles in the daylight" for everyone to see. He says:

> "As a Jew, I am devastated by these findings. The moral implications of this report should challenge us to the core. And I am deeply, deeply troubled that the primary response of our Jewish communal leadership is to attack the source of the report while saying absolutely nothing about its content."

He invites comments to his articles in his blog, and the comments keep on coming, showing readers struggling on their own on issues of, for instance, what the extent of their loyalty to Israel should be, where the borderline is between self-interest and ethical behavior, what should one chose, tribal answers or those that focus on larger issues, etc.

---

[26] Pg 120

Rabbi Rosen, a courageous man, gives no practical answers as to how Israel should handle practical problems. His solution is to step out of the compelling cocoon of Jewish community opinion and its code of honor, and instead be guided by the values of his own Jewish heritage that make possible the deep love for Israel and yet allow and even demand the critique of its policies. And thus he stands in solidarity with Palestinians and all others who are oppressed.

TRANSFORMATION OF THE JEWISH CHARACTER - GILAD ATZMON

Gilad Atzmon, in his book "The Wandering Who?" makes a study of Jewish Identity Politics. Atzmon, born in Israel, was a Zionists until his teenage years. He said that "supremacy was brewed into our souls, we gazed at the world through racist, chauvinistic binoculars", deeply convinced that the Jews were indeed the Chosen People.. Then, one night, he discovered jazz and suddenly saw himself as a part of a far greater family. A black man, Charlie Parker, whose music lifted him above his narrow self-absorbed Judeo-centric world, opened him to a more universal truth. But only after he joined the IDF and, in 1984, saw a huge detainment camp with Palestinian prisoners in the broiling heat of South Lebanon, did he fully break with the indoctrination of his youth. Now he is another one of those who examine the reasons, the roots and the deeper meaning of political developments, and he demands an honest process of self-reflection He also believes that humanism and universalism clashes with an adherence to a tribal tradition based on race and, in the Jewish case, on religion and history.

He differentiates between Jews (the people), Judaism (the religion) and Jewishness (the ideology). Those who call themselves Jews can be divided into three groups:

1. Those who follow Judaism
2. Those who regard themselves as human beings and happen to be of Jewish origin, and
3. Those who put their Jewishness over and above all of their other traits.[27]

It is the third category that Atzmon examines in detail. He goes back to Chaim Weizmann, one of the founders of Zionism and later the first Israeli President, who said:

> "There are no English, French, German or American Jews, but only Jews living in England, France, Germany or America."

Thus he defined the essence of Jewishness as a "primary quality". Being Jewish is the key element and the fundamental characteristics of a person. Everything else is secondary, and according to Atzmon, this assured that the Jew will always remain an alien. The early Zionist leader Vladimir Jabotinsky[28] said in 1904:

> "A Jew brought up among Germans may assume German customs, German words. He may be wholly imbued with that German fluid but the nucleus of his spiritual structure will always remain Jewish ,because his blood, his body, his physical racial type are Jewish."

---

[27] Atzmon, Gilad, *The Wandering Who*, pg 16

[28] Jabotinsky, Vladimir, *A Letter on Autonomy*, 1904

Gilad Atzmon, as a young secular Jews, wishes fervently for the possible transformation of the Jewish character with its "ethno-centric ideology driven by exclusiveness, exceptionalism, racial supremacy and a deep inherent inclination towards segregation" into a "civilized, authentic humanist collective". For that to happen, Atzmon believes that Israel must first stop being a Jewish State, but he fears that it is not able to bring about peace because of its inability to think in terms of harmony and reconciliation.

THE CASE AGAINST ISRAEL – MICHAEL NEUMANN

Michael Neumann, a son of German Jews, grew up in a family which had suffered greatly at the hands of the Nazis. Some of his relatives ended up in Palestine and are now Israeli citizens. So from early on, he was very involved in Israeli and Zionist aims and goals. He is one of the rare people who doesn't just see events, facts, arguments and agendas, but is able to cut through the fog of opinions, down to the kernels of truth illuminating basic moral and ethical ideas.

He is a Professor of Philosophy at Trent University in Ontario, Canada, and calls himself first and foremost a "moral and political philosopher". As such, he presents a clear moral analysis of the rights and wrongs of the conflict between the State of Israel and the Palestinian people, drawing the conclusion that Zionism originated the conflict and is responsible for its perpetuation.

I would like to report on and relate his arguments regarding only three issues, among many discussed in his book, namely:

1. Are the Jews a people?
2. Do the Jews have a right to the Land of Palestine?
3. What is the Final Solution? (Actual name of Chapter in Prof. Neumann's book)

Are the Jews a people?

The Declaration of the Establishment of the State of Israel from 1948 stated among other points:

"…the recognition by the United Nations of the right of the Jewish people to establish their State is irrevocable

…this right is the natural right of the Jewish people to be masters of their own fate, like all other nations, in their own sovereign State. "

It is often brought up in arguments that the Palestinians are not a people. In fact, they are a people with a common religion and culture, as well as a common language and long history, who live in a country called Palestine. Their forefathers farmed the land, owned property, raised children and lived in established towns and villages under the colonial administration of another power. The fact that, by historical chance, they did not have their own state doesn't mean that outsiders can come, control their territory and subjugate the people in it. America was a colony of Great Britain before it became the United

States, but the people who lived there had the right to reject the sovereign who tried to control their lives, even though they were not citizens of a state.

If it is true that Palestinians are not a people, the same can be said of Jews. Prof. Neumann calls the population of the Jewish State of Israel: an ethnically diverse people of which 20% are not even Jewish.

Not all Jews are religious – some are atheists, others are ultra-orthodox, orthodox, conservative, reform and Hassidic. There is also a range of followers of specific rabbis and their teachings. There are Sephardim from Spain and North Africa, Mizrahi from the Middle East and Ashkenazim from European Russia, the Ukraine and the Baltic States, as well as black Jews from Ethiopia. Immigrants tend to define themselves as Jewish first and Israelis second, while the people born in Israel (called "Sabras" after the fruit which is sweet on the inside and prickly on the outside) tend to define themselves as Israelis first and Jews second. Thousands of Russians Jewish immigrants are, strictly speaking, not Jewish at all since they are children of a Jewish father and a non-Jewish mother.[29] Immigrants from Ethiopia belong to an ancient people practicing a simpler kind of Judaism and are not accepted as full Jews, unless they undergo an orthodox conversion first.

Jews do not have a common language – not all speak Hebrew or Yiddish. They do not have a common culture because they have lived

---

[29] The original and current Jewish definition of a born Jew is someone whose mother is Jewish.

111

in a wide variety of countries all over the globe and, over time, adapted to different ways of life. They have differing culinary styles, different styles of dress, different kinds of music and differing customs. Thus they did not have a common history. Some were persecuted and others were full citizens of their countries with all its privileges. Zionism is a movement founded by Ashkenazim (German, Polish) atheists and is foreign to many Jews from other areas. The rate of intermarriage with Gentiles across the world is significant and alarming to many Jews.

Politically, some Jews were internationalists (communists, socialists, trade unionists). Others were faithful patriots of the countries they lived in, and yet others were not interested in any of these issues of political identity. Jews were largely citizens of other countries. They had no unifying leadership and no overriding shared political institutions.

It is also known that many outsiders converted to Judaism over the centuries, so one ethnicity does not fit "the Jews" as a whole. They are not "a race". Examinations shows that there is a considerable genetic relationship between the DNA of some Jews and Palestinians. Incorporated into the State are so-called Arabs who are really Palestinian and Muslim, as well as other minorities like Circassians, Druze, Alawites, Bedouins, Christians and even Samaritans, the remnants of the oldest component of the Israelite Kingdom, Samaria, with its focus on Jerusalem, destroyed by the Assyrians in 722 BCE, and who remained true to their religion as practiced then.

Israel may well be a state, but it is populated by an ethnically diverse people and cannot be called a "Jewish State" without relegating entire blocks of people to second-rate status.

Do the Jews have a right to the Land of Israel?

Historical claim. In pre-historic times Canaan was populated by a number of tribes, including Hittites, Amorites, Perizzites, Hivites, Girgashites, Jebusites, Philistines, Ammonites, Moabites, and Edomites. Among them, in the mountainous spine running down the length of today's Israel, a distinct tribe arose calling itself "Israelite" (meaning "Fighters for El", the Canaanite God also venerated by other tribes in Canaan.) Prof. Neumann doubts that it should matter whether some distant forefathers actually lived in the land 2000 to 3000 years ago. And, if they did, how can it be proven that they owned the land and did not conquer it, as both previous and subsequent conquerors have done? How can we ever determine the rightful owners of a property and, even further, how can we determine what property was owned by a certain "people"? How can it be determined whether Greeks, Turks or Chinese are the rightful owners of Greece, Turkey or China? How can we apply international law to nomadic tribes, migrations and wars that happened thousands of years ago? It is Prof. Neumann's opinion that "it really doesn't matter who inhabited

Palestine in the distant past; it would never give us a basis for deciding who should live there in the present".[30]

Biblical claim. It is in this area that the Zionist claim to the land is most dubious and controversial. It is a well accepted fact, and proven by excavations and the absence and presence of archaeological artifacts, that the "proof" of a Jewish right to the land is based, not on historical facts, but on myths, orally transmitted for hundreds of years, edited and adjusted to circumstances and only written down in the Torah between 550 – 300 BCE. Recent findings have been published by Israel Finkelstein, director of the archaeological institute at Tel Aviv University, and Neil Asher Silberman, director of a Belgian archaeological institute, in their book "*The Bible Unearthed: Archaeology's New Vision of Ancient Israel and the Origin of Its Sacred Texts*":

> "The historical saga contained in the Bible – from Abraham's encounter with God and his journey to Canaan, to Moses' deliverance of the children of Israel from bondage, to the rise and fall of the kingdoms of Israel and Judah – was not a miraculous revelation, but a brilliant product of the human imagination. ...Reexamination of the archaeological evidence ... points to a period of a few decades [in which a strong Israel existed] between around 835-800 BCE.[31]"

Prof. Neumann asks why the claims to the land should even be taken seriously. The biblical claim that God gave Israel to the Jews is not binding on all peoples in the world. It requires, as he states, "a belief in

---

[30] Michael Neumann, *The Case against Israel*, pg 69

[31] Finkelstein, Israel, and Silberman, Neil Asher "The Bible Unearthed", pgs 191, 202

the existence of a Jewish God and in the bible as the word of God". Belief in the right to the Land of Israel is, therefore, *contingent upon the loyalty to and belief in the Torah,* as well as a deeply-rooted conviction that Jews were chosen by God before all others.

It seems that Zionism has lost its claims of justification. But the Orthodox Jewish opposition, with its deep roots in Torah and Talmud, will simply disregard ethics, logic, archeology, historical scholarship, and international law and cling to the biblical myths that have long provided comfort and guidance in the shape of an unquestioned truth.

What is the Final Solution?

Prof. Neumann came to the conclusion that the Jews had no right to establish a state in Palestine. They had a right to flee there and find asylum during the dark times of the 20th century persecutions. But there is, as he says, a great difference between asylum and establishing a sovereign state. If I am trying to escape a lynch mob, I may have the right to invade your house to defend myself, but once that danger is past, I do not have the right to take over that house and your land and establish a sovereign state, expel you and your people, steal your property and make you a second-class population. As Prof. Neumann says, ethnic nationalism, fascism and racism were embodied in Nazism. We should have learned that these should not be the basis of any state.

Meanwhile, on an institutional basis, anti-Semitism has subsided. Jews live in dozens of countries with full civic rights and the right to practice their religion. Many have earned positions of great importance and influence in every country of their residence. The danger of another Holocaust has receded and hopefully will disappear entirely in the face of growing globalization. Immigration into Israel has also declined. In fact, more Israelis are leaving Israel for formerly hostile countries like Germany and Poland, integrating and becoming citizens of their forebears' respective countries.

Zionism built a state in the Middle East and gave a home to millions who had no home. Israel struggled for decades and has now reached a point where it is strong and self-sufficient, a military and nuclear power, a giant in education and research, a country with an infrastructure and institutions equivalent to those in any country in the world. While every country in the Middle East has given rise to Arab Spring demonstrations, Israeli demonstrations do not even mention the Palestinian occupation at all. They only deal with Jewish social justice concerns. This is an indication of how little the average Israeli is even aware of what is done to the suppressed minorities in its midst. It is Prof. Neumann's view that a greater injustice would be done if the State of Israel, even though built on false Zionist assumptions, would be dismantled or called illegal. It is legal now, it presents the "facts on the ground", just as America is legal now, even though the Native Americans were disenfranchised in the 19th century. Returning to the starting point is not possible, not in the USA and not in Israel, and not in any other countries built on historical conquest. Israel's existence, whether justifiable or not, is an accomplished-fact and need not be discussed and debated. But in the war of 1967 Israel conquered the West Bank and the Gaza Strip. Since then, Israel has constructed thousands of illegal settlements there, occupied by hundreds of thousands of Jewish settlers, mainly orthodox and ultra-orthodox, in anticipation of an eventual take-over and incorporation into the body of the State. Religious Jews see this as the fulfillment of God's wish for the Jews. This settlement policy is the main obstacle to peace.

As a result, the Palestinians in the Occupied Territories, whose land and water is taken away for settlements and who suffer severe hardship under military occupation, have only one path of action open to them: violent resistance. This is usually answered by Israel with disproportionate force and military intervention. The illegal occupation and its implications give great pain to Israelis of conscience, whether Zionists or not. However, there is another option, namely unilateral withdrawal from the Occupied Territories. As Prof Neumann writes, this "requires no negotiations, no change in Palestinian attitudes, no trust and no improvement in the effectiveness of the Palestinian Authority."

Israel, in its strength as a State with power and influence, does not have to fear war with its neighbors, if peaceful relations exist and its increasing diplomatic isolation has ended.

What would be the alternative? The illegal occupation of the Territories does violate many Jews' sense of ethics, as it contradicts their highest values. On a practical level, demographic studies suggest that Palestinians with their greater birthrate will outnumber Jews in a few short years. Is Israel willing to govern a country under Apartheid in the Occupied Territories, like South Africa? Is it willing to give up the idea of a Jewish State and consolidate the area into one Democratic State for all its citizens, including Jews and Arabs and every other resident?

THE ONE-STATE SOLUTION - JOEL KOVEL

Joel Kovel was the son of Jewish immigrants from the pogrom-ridden Ukraine, who arrived in the United States early in the 20th century and made a life here. He was influenced early on by his father, a tragic and lonely figure who developed extreme right wing views and even supported some fascist causes, for example, that of the dictator Francisco Franco of Spain. He hated Zionism because he thought, mistakenly, that it was socialist, and correctly, that it would entail divided loyalty to his beloved United States. He was also influenced by his free-thinking aunt Betty who questioned every kind of conformism. Her early death and his relatives' condemnation of her life's decisions hardened Prof. Kovel's heart against what he viewed as hypocrisy inside his ancestral religion which had already undergone a period of deep questioning and doubt.

Jewish chauvinism and sense of entitlement led eventually to his critique of Zionism. He believes that mankind must find its expression in an infinite, universal and inclusive existence. A state for the exclusive ownership of one religion, be it Jewish, Christian, Islamic or Hindu, is, in his opinion, an unjust nightmare. And Israel, the State created by Zionism, exhibits tribal, exclusive, imperialist, racist, and apartheid traits. He sees that Zionism is faulty at its core and need a reformation in favor of a universal State for Jews, Arabs and all citizens, in order to bring Jews into the family of nations. .

In describing the early Israelites, the seer Balaam, in the fourth book of Numbers, states: "Behold, it is a people dwelling apart, not counting itself among the nations." This choice to live as a "people apart", based no doubt on the conviction of being chosen by God above all others, set up a dynamic of reaction and counter-reaction feeding exclusivity, segregation, and prejudice. As Prof. Kovel states, the origin of antisemitism can be found in this dialectic as well as in the reaction to anti-Semitism known as Zionism, the longing for a Jewish homeland.

To go against this historical belief of Jewish chosenness and apartness was always dangerous. Jesus, who lived and died a Jew, wanted to change the prevailing Jewish culture by teaching a universal "vision of justice" by a God who values every human being. As Prof. Kovel says, Jesus was asking for trouble, and got it. The Talmudic tradition, itself shaped by persecution and ghettoization, increased the chasm between

Jews and others by stating, repeatedly and in different forms, that only Jews are considered truly human.

The tribal mindset of the Jewish people manifested itself in a modern, militarized and aggressive state structure, exhibiting all the signs of historical Jewish tribalism. But the victims of the modern Zionist state had nothing to do with past sufferings visited upon Jews. It was European countries that expelled Jews during the Middle Ages. It was Poland and Russia that created pogroms, and it was Germany that caused the Holocaust. Today however, it is the Palestinians, inside the land of their own birth, who are dispossessed, persecuted, occupied and made refugees at the hands of the Zionist State of Israel, which considers them subhuman.

For Judaism to regain its soul, according to Prof. Kovel, Zionism must be overcome. A "two-state" solution in which both Israel and Palestine live side by side in their own states will not suffice. What is needed is a single state for all citizens, based on the principle that all human beings have inherent worth and dignity, deserving justice and equality. In such a country, no one would be inherently more worthy than another, and no previous suffering could legitimize injustice. Racism would be eliminated by regarding all citizens as universally chosen.

No worthwhile accomplishment is easy, and a one-state solution requires the overcoming of differences. According to Prof. Kovel, in the case of "two polities so radically opposed and yet so intertwined", this could either be a bi-national state in which Jews and Arabs coexist, or – more advanced – a state in which people still recognize their national identity, but overcome this through inclusion in a larger whole, thereby also overcoming chauvinism. Each group's identity is thereby freed from national or tribal limitations, but retains a connection with its cultural identity through tradition and memory. Prof. Kovel calls it a secular-universal state, bridging its integration into the Arab Middle East, instead of remaining a colonial transplant in a hostile and culturally different environment.

Prof. Kovel, a psychiatrist, social activist, academic and writer, has a number of books and articles to his credit. He was appointed to the Alger Hiss Chair of Social Studies at Bard College in 1988. His contract was terminated in 2009. In Prof. Kovel's view this was not for pedagogic or intellectual considerations, but, as he remarks: "for political values, principally stemming from differences between myself and the Bard administration on the issue of Zionism."

REMEMBRANCE AND FORGIVENESS - MARK H. ELLIS

Marc H. Ellis was born to Jewish parents in Miami, Florida, and is currently a professor and Director of the Center for American and Jewish Studies at Baylor University. He has written 15 books about Judaism and matters relating to the history and future of Israel and is considered one of the most influential Jewish thinkers of his generation, demonstrating, as Noam Chomsky said, "great courage, integrity and insight". His book *"Israel and Palestine – Out of the Ashes – The Search for Jewish Identity in the Twenty-First Century"* is dense, deep and rich in insight and explanations. I would like to deal here with only some of his topics, namely prophesy, memory and forgiveness, as well as the Holocaust and its connection to the State of Israel.

Influenced by the ethical tradition inherent in Judaism and changes in Jewish life after the Holocaust and the founding of Israel, Prof Ellis sought to make sense of the past and to retain the Jewish ethics so valuable to him, in a world where multiple forces collectively effected change. In his studies, he came into contact with Christian Liberation

Theology, which focused on caring and working for justice for the poor and downtrodden. Concurrently, he was disturbed by the increasing militarization of both America and Israel and the fate of the Palestinians, who had been dispossessed by the creation of the Jewish State. He developed insight into Jewish-Christian-Muslim relations in the modern world and found acceptance in a wide array of universities and institutes, whose aim it is to seek justice and peace while working within faith-based religious and national identities. He also experienced attacks from those who perceived insights as an attack on Israel itself.

To Prof. Ellis, a life that does not transcend self and the material, and does not recognize a higher and more encompassing reality, is not worth living. He believes that prophets speak within their historical context, but also speak to a wounded humanity and those who see the pain but don't know how to express it. This requires a vision and conviction of mission but also courage to follow the dictates of one's conscience. For him the prophet expresses a breadth of insight over the confusion of everyday detail. Prof. Ellis clearly speaks with a prophetic voice, hoping to awaken a perception that justice must be at the core of society and its institutions.

Prof. Ellis sees that the Judaism he was born into has been radically changed into one in which the Holocaust is tied up closely with the State of Israel and its newly-found power. He is searching for a new Jewish identity, built on the ethics of a Jewish life which he treasured, and seeking to use that vision to spread the word of a better and more just world.

Judaism's sense of history and very existence is built on memory, an imperative for all Jews and central to Jewish identity, culture and religion. However, it focuses on exclusivity and chosenness in relationship to God and His protection. It also remembers, first and foremost, Jewish suffering through the ages and especially, most recently, during the Holocaust. This focus on Jewish suffering disconnects Jews from the wider world and creates a fearful anticipation that "the Holocaust will happen again". Some Jewish scholars would like to permanently include a commemoration of the Holocaust into the Jewish liturgical calendar.

But holding on to the memory of the suffering, as exemplified by the Holocaust, leaves little room for knowing the suffering which is caused to other people, namely the Palestinians. Prof. Ellis insists that "a country that wants to be part of the community of democratic, law-abiding countries cannot justify such a blatant violation of legal principles and basic human values."[32] He brings in Irena Klepfisz, a survivor of the Warsaw Ghetto and the Holocaust itself, who rose above her own suffering to see and condemn the destruction of the ordinary life of Palestinians through the formation of Israel. She demanded that Palestinian suffering be remembered also.

---

[32] Page 42

125

One day, during one of his lectures, Prof. Ellis was confronted by a Catholic nun who accused him of hating Hitler "in his heart". This started a contemplation of the difference between Christianity (which teaches to forgive those who forgive their enemies) and Judaism (which holds on to grievances and teaches never to forget)[33]. It was Jesus who was nailed on the cross and said: "Father forgive them, because they don't know what they are doing."

Can Jews forgive the Holocaust and the massive scale of their own suffering? These wounds remain as open sores and underlie today's violence perpetrated by Israel on another innocent people. What would happen if Germans were forgiven for the Holocaust? Prof. Ellis asks: would they be able to live with the memory of the suffering they caused and turn towards healing other people's pain and empower victims everywhere?

Would forgiveness also free Jews to let go of the darkness of the past to work towards healing themselves and others?

Prof. Ellis says that this revolutionary forgiveness, even though it is Christian in inspiration, is also Jewish. It embodies at its deepest core the Jewish demand for justice and the possibility of forming a new social and political entity built on inclusive and universal human values.

Forgiving, like a stone thrown into a pond, creates circles of healing and hope for a better future.

---

[33] Luke 23, 34

Dr. Ellis is currently under internal investigation at Baylor University in what looks like an attempt to silence a Jewish voice of dissent.

A COURAGEOUS VISION –
AVRAHAM BURG

Avraham Burg, the son of a German-Jewish father and a Jewish mother from Hebron, was born in Israel and is a proud and courageous citizen of his country. He has an impeccable resumé. As a young man he served as a lieutenant in the paratroopers division of the Israeli Defense Forces, became a Leader in the Labor Party, member of the Knesset and eventually the Speaker of the Knesset. After resignation from the Knesset, he was the Chairman of the Jewish Agency and the World Zionist Organization, working on behalf of reparations for Holocaust survivors.

Very early in his career, he questioned national dogmas and examined them in light of universal paradigms. It seemed obvious to him that "the Shoah", as he calls the Holocaust, is at the basis of Israel's national consciousness and infecting that of the entire Western World in the process. It so dominates every aspect of Israeli life that it colors the view of the past, present and future. The poor, half-starved people, who washed ashore in the newly formed State of Israel after the end of WWII, knew themselves to be victims in a world that had tried its best to kill them all. That fact was so burned into every Israeli's mind that it became a holy mission never to forget, never to get weak again, never to be dominated by anybody else. Both the building of the Jewish State and the Holocaust became two inseparably intertwined events. Having survived the Holocaust generated a sense of victimhood, but also a sense of pride. It led to a conviction that as victims, they know what path to choose.

Over time, relations with Germany were restored, allowing Israel to accept reparations for the Jewish victims, as well as substantial sums for the building of the new State of Israel (without which, this undertaking would have been much more difficult).

Somehow, the Nazis who originally had caused this trauma, receded into the background while the Arabs came to the forefront, portrayed as worse than the Germans, seemingly re-incarnating the Nazi spirit into the Arab body. Mr. Burg describes in detail how this transfer of anger and revenge took place, from one people to another, and how the Shoah, directly or indirectly, caused the Palestinian refugee problem and the poisonous relationship Israel has with the displaced population.

Mr. Burg examines the various other "holocausts" caused and suffered by different people in the last few hundred years, pointing to a long list of suffering by innocents. It is estimated that between 1900 and 1987, for instance, the unimaginable number of 169 billion people perished in genocides, including those in China, Russia and Turkey. To this must be added, after 1987, mass murder in Rwanda, Yugoslavia, East Timor and elsewhere. And what about the mass killing of Natives and slaves, the horrific toll caused by racism in America, and the extermination of native peoples caused by colonial racism in India and Africa during the last century? Mr. Burg demands that Jews take a stand on the side of all persecuted. He does not see Jews and their national interests, but human beings and universal concerns. He demands a moral position, even if it is against evil in oneself. Mr. Burg removes from the Shoah its sanctity and draws attention to its use for Israel's political benefit. When confronted with inhumanity to men, he uses what power he has to speak up. This is his dual responsibility as a human being and as a Jew.

Israel has appropriated the Holocaust as its exclusive property along with its position as a victim, not recognizing that the situation has changed and Jewish victimhood can no longer co-exist with Israel's position in the modern world. Never before has World Jewry had their own state, recognition among the countries of the world and power in international affairs. In order to belong to the circle of nations of the world, Mr. Burg says, Israel needs to change its worldview. The Shoah at this time is Israel's main asset, leveling immediate charges of anti-Semitism when any criticism is brought forth.

In his book "The Holocaust is over – we must rise from its Ashes" Mr. Burg presents a soaring vision of what it means to be "a light upon all nations" and a realization of what it means to be Jewish in the best sense. The current Holocaust culture, based on memory and its reinforcement, is certain to perpetuate the "cycle of pathology" for future generations.

Holocaust Memorial Day, the day of the Warsaw ghetto uprising, should become both a commemoration of Jewish heroism in the face of the impending destruction, and of resistance to crimes against all humanity committed in the future..

The day of the liberation of Auschwitz should be celebrated, not just in commemoration of the suffering of Jews, but of humanity as a whole. Israelis and Israel's Arab citizens should stand united, both grieving in their own pain and bonding in a new human obligation. That day should inspire the promise of "No more". He says: "no more violence, no more xenophobia, no more discrimination, and no more racism. In school we will study other people's holocausts; we will understand the origins of violence and aggression and the ways to eradicate them; we will fight tyranny and commit to justice, equality, and peace"[34]. Mr. Burg expresses, in a different way, what had been my mantra: the Holocaust should never happen again to Jews, but also not to any persons of any religious, national, ethnic, or racial origin.

More importantly, Israelis should stand, side by side with the nations of the civilized world, in a struggle against hatred wherever it raises its ugly head, converting personal wounds into "a cure for all humanity".

---

[34] Burg, Avraham, pg 232

This will necessitate a new Israeli identity and a connection to the soul of Judaism which shares its fate and its values with others. We may be children of Abraham and Sarah, Mr. Burg says, but we are all children of Adam and Eve.

Mr. Burg, with a prophetic voice, lays out a vision demanding nothing less than the rearrangement of a long-entrenched worldview, including one point considered indispensable: the act of forgiving Germany. He expects that many will not be willing to do that. But it is his hope that others understand that Israel cannot ever be free until this happens, - until it recognizes that suffering belongs to mankind and is not owned by one people. Germany itself, aware of its responsibility to atone for the crimes of the past, will change "the picture of the world's evil and paint it with goodness". For Avraham Burg, the best interest of the human race is at stake.

THE FUTURE OF ISRAEL - LIBERAL ZIONISTS SPEAK OUT

One of the leading US blogs, the Huffington Post, invited Liberal Zionists to submit essays which would express their relationship to the State of Israel and their expectations of what Israel's future should be like. Without exception these Jews, born in Israel or brought up in other countries, living in Israel now or still residents abroad, accept the existence of the Jewish State of Israel as necessary and absolutely vital to the Jews of the world, who need a state of their own where they can feel secure and free. How liberating, to finally not feel as a minority but empowered among one's own people!

In their own country, they could see themselves "as part of a universal movement aimed at making the world a better place, taking care of the weak in society, striving for a more egalitarian society", as one person wrote. One writer expected "a feeling of social solidarity and a sense of community." "A place of justice, one that lives up to Israel's Declaration of Independence," says another. One speaks of her dream of peace, equality and justice and feels torn between her commitment to Zionism and estrangement from her homeland. Another writer is seeking "the moral logic of the Jewish State with coexistence between Palestinians and Israeli Jews." There was hope that Zionism would look for the middle road, avoid both messianism and territorial gains, but instead promoting a "constant, gradual progress and reconciliation between Jews and themselves, as well as between Jews and Arabs, including full equality and integration of Israel's minority citizens as a test of Israel's democracy".

No one mentioned the inherent myths of Zionism, which promised "a land without people to a people without land", as it is now quite obvious, that the land had previously been densely settled by other people. The pogroms and the Holocaust were "seared into their souls" during their growing years and reinforced the absolute necessity for the Zionist goal of Jewish Statehood. It was also not mentioned that the assumed right to a homeland in Israel was anchored in ancient tribal myths which the Torah recorded as historical facts. The archaeological discoveries of recent years are said to gnaw at the justification for Zionism, but both Fundamentalists and Liberal Zionists fully accept the historical justifications as presented in the Torah. Zionists' identity, their historical perspective, core beliefs and their pride is defined by Zionism. All authors accepted as absolutely necessary the historical necessity of Israel's creation and continuing

136

existence. And most writers believe that Israel must, by necessity, be a Jewish State. To believe anything else would be unbearable.

But what became of this Zionist dream?

While some authors failed to mention any problems with illegal Jewish settlements in the Occupied Territories and the suppression of another people, the difficulties inherent in a Jewish Democratic State with non-Jewish citizens, the messianic power of the ultra-national fundamentalists seriously disturbed many as the cracks they can see widening. "The occupation is a cancer that is eating us up", says one, "deeply troubled by Israel's policies" such as expanding settlements, appropriating Palestinian land, and the heavy-handed restriction on Palestinian movement and trade. One speaks about "tribalism" and fearing the actions of the ultra-Orthodox, a small but growing part of the population which had been given extraordinary political powers when the State was founded. Another feels that Israel's security is more threatened from within than without by the anti-democratic and even racist political culture that has emerged in Israel as a result of the occupation. All of this creates a serious unease, a "dis-ease", in liberal-thinking Jews, humanist and religious alike, residents in Israel as well as other places, to the extent, as one author reports, that thousands of Israelis leave every year for other countries. The blog "abrahamonline" writes that an estimated 70 per cent of Israelis are thought to have a second passport, with Germany the most favoured place for alternative citizenship -- a surprising sign, seemingly at odds with Zionist and

Israeli history. German officials say that more than 100,000 such passports have been granted since 2000.

Almost all writers agreed that Israel's continued independence rests on a resolution with Palestinians, an end to the debilitating animosity and bloodshed. This is not entirely for the welfare of the Palestinians. In fact, there is great concern for Israel's longevity as a Jewish state, since it is estimated that the population numbers of both people will reach parity soon and in the future will show a sharp rise in Palestine numbers due to the higher Palestinian birth rate. After years of pushing Jewish settlement in the occupied territories and refusing to agree to a Palestinian state, the possibility of a one-state solution for Jews and Arabs is viewed with great anguish. It would destroy the coveted Jewish character of Israel, so there is a growing consensus that a Palestinian state is not in Israel's and the global Jewish community's self-interest.

One writer describes his Zionism as a secular nationalism, speaking about the twofold character of the Jewish people. Israel is a nation and also a so-called community of faith. He postulates that statehood "requires that the Jewish state should be an expression of the people, not of the faith". Is this an attempt at "separation of church and state?"

A large part of the population apparently views the political situation in Israel as great anguish that "rends their souls". They desire a Jewish state that "more honorably addresses its own Palestinian population, that more effectively reforms its educational system, and more energetically pursues social justice in line with the Jewish values which they treasure."

Reading through the dozens of essays, three possibilities arise, all of them painful:

1. Continuation of the *status quo* with ultra-nationalists expanding the settlement effort to eventually incorporate the territories into the State of Israel. Israel is a Jewish state, but not a democratic state. In reality, as an apartheid state, generating hate among the suppressed, it will find it impossible to take a place in the community of the world's nations. The Children of the Holocaust cannot continue to rely on tales of suffering, without realizing their own abusive roles.

2. A two-state solution with negotiated land swaps in addition to relocation of settlers into Israel proper, perhaps as part of a confederation with Jordan. One author says: "Let there be no mistake: two states for two peoples is not an easy solution. It is fraught with complexity. Where, exactly, shall the borders be? What, exactly, will be the regulations covering access from one of the two states to the other? What about Jerusalem? What about security, and the consequences if the opponents of partition, from whichever side, act out or seek to subvert the arrangement?"

3. Given the trajectory of Israel's *status quo*, it is unlikely that Palestinians will continue to be motivated to work for a two-state solution, as population parity approaches. Logically, they would then push for "one-person-one vote": one universal state for all its citizens, Jewish and Arab alike, with equal rights for all. Israel would finally be democratic, but no longer "Jewish".

As Avraham Burg writes in his book *The Holocaust is Over – We must Rise from its Ashes,* Israel needs a vision "demanding nothing less than the rearrangement of a long-entrenched worldview". It is not enough to use band-aids like "stop teaching hate" or "try to consider the rights of others". The basis for any positive future must be defined by a willingness to examine and question the current assumptions -- biblical, historical, mythical, cultural, Zionist -- all based on purely tribal terms. Clearly, that change would serve the best interests of not only Israel, but also the future of regional and global security.

From its beginnings, was Zionism just an impossible dream? And now, is Israel a dream, vanishing in the face of difficult choices? Today, Israel is stronger than ever before, with both an educated populace and institutions comparable to other advanced nations, characterized by a high degree of development and culture. The question remains however: will it overcome its factiousness and self-absorption, the myths and memories of its past and the right-wing resistance, to look to the future and work towards an Israel finally embraced by the world community of nations, exhibiting Jewish values of justice and ethics and being a blessing for mankind? That is my hope. Then we actually might have peace in the Middle East.

Attachments

ABOUT THE AUTHOR

Inge Etzbach was born in Germany in 1932. Because of her experiences during WWII and the Hitler years she came to feel a deep connection with Israel and Palestine.

When her youngest child started school, Inge entered Queens College and studied Philosophy, graduating in 1985 with a B.A. in Philosophy and in 1991 with a M.A. in Political Science. She is also an ordained Interfaith Minister. In 1987 she spent several months in Israel, working in a kibbutz and as a volunteer in the Israeli Army. Over the next few years, she participated in several Peace-Building Delegations, interacting with Israeli and Palestinian officials and ordinary citizens in Israel and the West Bank and participating in Mideast Workshops. She also travelled extensively in the area on her own.

She has three grown children and lives in New York City and Copake Falls, NY

DECONSTRUCTING THE WALLS OF JERICHO

Article originally published in Ha'aretz in October of 1999

By Prof. Ze'ev Herzog
Tel-Aviv University

Following 70 years of intensive excavations in the Land of Israel, archaeologists have found out: The patriarchs' acts are legendary stories, we did not sojourn in Egypt or make an exodus, we did not conquer the land. Neither is there any mention of the empire of David and Solomon. Those who take an interest have known these facts for years, but Israel is a stubborn people and doesn't want to hear about it.

This is what archaeologists have learned from their excavations in the Land of Israel: the Israelites were never in Egypt, did not wander in the desert, did not conquer the land in a military campaign and did not pass it on to the 12 tribes of Israel. Perhaps even harder to swallow is that the united monarchy of David and Solomon, which is described by the Bible as a regional power, was at most a small tribal kingdom. And it will come as an unpleasant shock to many that the God of Israel, YHWH, had a female consort and that the early Israelite religion adopted monotheism only in the waning period of the monarchy and not at Mount Sinai.

Most of those who are engaged in scientific work in the interlocking spheres of the Bible, archaeology and the history of the Jewish people and who once went into the field looking for proof to corroborate the Bible story now agree that the historic events relating to the stages of the Jewish people's emergence are radically different from what that story tells.

What follows is a short account of the brief history of archaeology, with the emphasis on the crises and the big bang, so to speak, of the past decade. The critical question of this archaeological revolution has not yet trickled down into public consciousness, but it cannot be ignored.

Inventing the Bible Stories

The archaeology of Palestine developed as a science at a relatively late date, in the late 19th and early 20th century, in tandem with the archaeology of the imperial cultures of Egypt, Mesopotamia, Greece and Rome. Those resource-intensive powers were the first target of the researchers, who were looking for impressive evidence from the past, usually in the service of the big museums in London, Paris and Berlin. That stage effectively passed over Palestine, with its fragmented geographical diversity. The conditions in ancient Palestine were inhospitable for the development of an extensive kingdom, and certainly no showcase projects such as the Egyptian shrines or the Mesopotamian palaces could have been established there. In fact, the archaeology of Palestine was not engendered at the initiative of museums but arose from religious motives.

The main push behind archaeological research in Palestine was the country's relationship with the Holy Scriptures. The first excavators in Jericho and Shechem (Nablus) were biblical researchers who were looking for the remains of the cities cited in the Bible. Archaeology assumed momentum with the activity of William Foxwell Albright, who mastered the archaeology, history and languages of the Land of Israel and the ancient Near East. Albright, an American whose father was a priest of Chilean descent, began excavating in Palestine in the 1920's. His stated approach was that archaeology was the principal scientific means to refute the critical claims against the historical veracity of the Bible stories, particularly those of the Wellhausen school in Germany.

The school of biblical criticism that developed in Germany beginning in the second half of the 19th century, of which Julius Wellhausen was a leading figure, challenged the historicity of the Bible stories and

145

claimed that biblical historiography was formulated, and in large measure actually 'invented', during the Babylonian exile. Bible scholars, the Germans in particular, claimed that the history of the Hebrews, as a consecutive series of events beginning with Abraham, Isaac, and Jacob, and proceeding through the passage to Egypt, the enslavement and the exodus, and ending with the conquest of the land and the settlement of the tribes of Israel, was no more than a later reconstruction of events with a theological purpose.

Albright believed that the Bible is a historical document, which, although it had gone through several editing stages, nevertheless basically reflected the ancient reality. He was convinced that if the ancient remains of Palestine were uncovered, they would furnish unequivocal proof of the historical truth of the events relating to the Jewish people in its land.

The biblical archaeology that developed following Albright and his pupils brought about a series of extensive digs at the important biblical tells: Megiddo, Lachish, Gezer, Shechem (Nablus), Jericho, Jerusalem, Ai, Giveon, Beit She'an, Beit Shemesh, Hazor, Ta'anach and others. The way was straight and clear: every new finding contributed to the building of a harmonious picture of the past. The archaeologists, who enthusiastically adopted the biblical approach, set out on a quest to unearth the 'biblical period': the period of the patriarchs, the Canaanite cities that were destroyed by the Israelites as they conquered the land, the boundaries of the 12 tribes, the sites of the settlement period, characterized by 'settlement pottery', the 'gates of Solomon' at Hazor, Megiddo and Gezer, 'Solomon's stables' (or Ahab's), 'King Solomon's mines' at Timnaóand there are some who are still hard at work and have found Mount Sinai (at Mount Karkoum in the Negev) or Joshua's altar at Mount Ebal.

The Crisis

Slowly, cracks began to appear in the picture. Paradoxically, a situation was created in which the glut of findings began to undermine the historical credibility of the biblical descriptions instead of reinforcing them. A crisis stage is reached when the theories within the framework

146

of the general thesis are unable to solve an increasingly large number of anomalies.

The explanations become ponderous and inelegant, and the pieces do not fit together smoothly. Here are a few examples of how the harmonious picture collapsed. Patriarchal Age: The researchers found it difficult to reach agreement on which archaeological period matched the Patriarchal Age. When did Abraham, Isaac and Jacob live? When was the Cave of Machpelah (Tomb of the Patriarchs in Hebron) bought in order to serve as the burial place for the patriarchs and the matriarchs? According to the biblical chronology, Solomon built the Temple 480 years after the exodus from Egypt (1 Kings 6:1). To that we have to add 430 years of the stay in Egypt (Exodus 12:40) and the vast lifetimes of the patriarchs, producing a date in the 21st century BCE for Abraham's move to Canaan. However, no evidence has been unearthed that can sustain this chronology. Albright argued in the early 1960s in favor of assigning the wanderings of Abraham to the Middle Bronze Age (22nd -20th centuries BCE). However, Benjamin Mazar, the father of the Israeli branch of biblical archaeology, proposed identifying the historic background of the Patriarchal Age a thousand years later, in the 11th century BCE, which would place it in the 'settlement period'. Others rejected the historicity of the stories and viewed them as ancestral legends that were told in the period of the Kingdom of Judea. In any event, the consensus began to break down. The Exodus from Egypt, the wanderings in the desert and Mount Sinai: The many Egyptian documents that we have make no mention of the Israelites' presence in Egypt and are also silent about the events of the Exodus. Many documents do mention the custom of nomadic shepherds to enter Egypt during periods of drought and hunger and to camp at the edges of the Nile Delta. However, this was not a solitary phenomenon: such events occurred frequently over thousands of years and were hardly exceptional. Generations of researchers tried to locate Mount Sinai and the encampments of the tribes in the desert. Despite these intensive efforts, not even one site has been found that can match the biblical account.

The power of tradition has now led some researchers to 'discover' Mount Sinai in the northern Hijaz or, as already mentioned, at Mount

147

Karkoum in the Negev. The central events in the history of the Israelites are not corroborated in documents external to the Bible or in archaeological findings. Most historians today agree that at best, the stay in Egypt and the exodus events occurred among a few families and that their private story was expanded and 'nationalized' to fit the needs of theological ideology.

The conquest:

One of the formative events of the people of Israel in biblical historiography is the story of how the land was conquered from the Canaanites. Yet extremely serious difficulties have cropped up precisely in the attempts to locate the archaeological evidence for this story. Repeated excavations by various expeditions at Jericho and Ai, the two cities whose conquest is described in the greatest detail in the Book of Joshua, have proved very disappointing. Despite the excavators' efforts, it emerged that in the late part of the 13th century BCE, at the end of the Late Bronze Age, which is the agreed period for the conquest, there were no cities in either tell, and of course no walls that could have been toppled. Naturally, explanations were offered for these anomalies. Some claimed that the walls around Jericho were washed away by rain, while others suggested that earlier walls had been used; and, as for Ai, it was claimed that the original story actually referred to the conquest of nearby Beit El and was transferred to Ai by later redactors.

Biblical scholars suggested a quarter of a century ago that the conquest stories be viewed as etiological legends and no more. But as more and more sites were uncovered and it emerged that the places in question died out or were simply abandoned at different times, the conclusion that there is no factual basis for the biblical story about the conquest by Israelite tribes in a military campaign led by Joshua was bolstered. The Canaanite cities: The Bible magnifies the strength and the fortifications of the Canaanite cities that were conquered by the Israelites: 'great cities with walls sky-high' (Deuteronomy 9:1). In practice, all the sites that have been uncovered turned up remains of unfortified settlements, which in most cases consisted of a few structures or the ruler's palace

148

rather than a genuine city. The urban culture of Palestine in the Late Bronze Age disintegrated in a process that lasted hundreds of years and did not stem from military conquest.

Moreover, the biblical description is unfamiliar with the geopolitical reality in Palestine. Palestine was under Egyptian rule until the middle of the 12th century BCE. The Egyptians' administrative centers were located in Gaza, Yaffo and Beit She'an. Egyptian presence has also been discovered in many locations on both sides of the Jordan River. This striking presence is not mentioned in the biblical account, and it is clear that it was unknown to the author and his editors. The archaeological findings blatantly contradict the biblical picture: the Canaanite cities were not 'great,' were not fortified and did not have 'sky-high walls.' The heroism of the conquerors, the few versus the many and the assistance of the God who fought for his people are a theological reconstruction lacking any factual basis. Origin of the Israelites: The conclusions drawn from episodes in the emergence of the people of Israel in stages, taken together, gave rise to a discussion of the bedrock question: the identity of the Israelites. If there is no evidence for the exodus from Egypt and the desert journey, and if the story of the military conquest of fortified cities has been refuted by archaeology, who, then, were these Israelites? The archaeological findings did corroborate one important fact: in the early Iron Age (beginning some time after 1200 BCE), the stage that is identified with the 'settlement period', hundreds of small settlements were established in the area of the central hill region of the Land of Israel, inhabited by farmers who worked the land or raised sheep. If they did not come from Egypt, what is the origin of these settlers? Israel Finkelstein, professor of archaeology at Tel Aviv University, has proposed that these settlers were the pastoral shepherds who wandered in this hill area throughout the Late Bronze Age (graves of these people have been found, without settlements). According to his reconstruction, in the Late Bronze Age (which preceded the Iron Age) the shepherds maintained a barter economy of meat in exchange for grains with the inhabitants of the valleys. With the disintegration of the urban and agricultural system in the lowlands, the nomads were forced to produce their own grains, and hence the incentive for stable settlements.

149

The name 'Israel' is mentioned in a single Egyptian document from the period of Merneptah, king of Egypt, dating from 1208 BCE: 'Plundered is Canaan with every evil, Ascalon is taken, Gezer is seized, Yenoam has become as though it never was, Israel is desolated, its seed is not.' Merneptah refers to the country by its Canaanite name and mentions several cities of the kingdom, along with a non-urban ethnic group. According to this evidence, the term 'Israel' was given to one of the population groups that resided in Canaan toward the end of the Late Bronze Age, apparently in the central hill region, in the area where the Kingdom of Israel would later be established.

A Kingdom With No Name

The united monarchy: Archaeology was also the source that brought about a shift regarding the reconstruction of the reality in the period known as the 'united monarchy' of David and Solomon'. The Bible describes this period as the zenith of the political, military and economic power of the people of Israel in ancient times. In the wake of David's conquests, the empire of David and Solomon stretched from the Euphrates River to Gaza ('For he controlled the whole region west of the Euphrates, from Tiphsah to Gaza, all the kings west of the Euphrates,' 1 Kings 5:4). The archaeological findings at many sites show that the construction projects attributed to this period were meager in scope and power.

The three cities of Hazor, Megiddo and Gezer, which are mentioned among Solomon's construction enterprises, have been excavated extensively at the appropriate layers. Only about half of Hazor's upper city was fortified, covering an area of only 30 dunams (7.5 acres), out of a total area of 700 dunams which was settled in the Bronze Age. At Gezer there was apparently only a citadel surrounded by a casemate wall covering a small area, while Megiddo was not fortified with a wall. The picture becomes even more complicated in the light of the excavations conducted in Jerusalem, the capital of the united monarchy. Large sections of the city have been excavated over the past 150 years. The digs have turned up impressive remnants of the cities from the Middle Bronze Age and from Iron Age II (the period of the

Kingdom of Judea). No remains of buildings have been found from the period of the united monarchy (even according to the agreed chronology), only a few pottery shards. Given the preservation of the remains from earlier and later periods, it is clear that Jerusalem in the time of David and Solomon was a small city, perhaps with a small citadel for the king, but in any event it was not the capital of an empire as described in the Bible. This small chiefdom is the source of the title 'Beth David' mentioned in later Aramean and Moabite inscriptions. The authors of the biblical account knew Jerusalem in the 8th century BCE, with its wall and the rich culture of which remains have been found in various parts of the city, and projected this picture back to the age of the united monarchy. Presumably, Jerusalem acquired its central status after the destruction of Samaria, its northern rival, in 722 BCE.

The archaeological findings dovetail well with the conclusions of the critical school of biblical scholarship. David and Solomon were the rulers of tribal kingdoms that controlled small areas: the former in Hebron and the latter in Jerusalem. Concurrently, a separate kingdom began to form in the Samaria hills, which finds expression in the stories about Saul's kingdom. Israel and Judea were from the outset two separate, independent kingdoms, and at times were in an adversarial relationship. Thus, the great united monarchy is an imaginary historiosophic creation, which was composed during the period of the Kingdom of Judea at the earliest. Perhaps the most decisive proof of this is that we do not know the name of this kingdom.

YHWH and his Consort

How many gods, exactly, did Israel have? Together with the historical and political aspects, there are also doubts as to the credibility of the information about belief and worship. The question about the date at which monotheism was adopted by the kingdoms of Israel and Judea arose with the discovery of inscriptions in ancient Hebrew that mention a pair of gods: YHWH and his Asherath. At two sites, Kuntilet Ajrud in the southwestern part of the Negev hill region, and Khirbet el-Kom in the Judea piedmont, Hebrew inscriptions have been found that mention 'YHWH and his Asherah', 'YHWH Shomron and his Asherah', 'YHWH Teman and his Asherah'. The authors were familiar with a pair of gods, YHWH and his consort Asherah, and send blessings in the couple's name. These inscriptions, from the 8th century BCE, raise the possibility that monotheism, as a state religion, is actually an innovation of the period of the Kingdom of Judea, following the destruction of the Kingdom of Israel.

The archaeology of the Land of Israel is completing a process that amounts to a scientific revolution in its field. It is ready to confront the findings of biblical scholarship and of ancient history as an equal discipline. But at the same time, we are witnessing a fascinating phenomenon in that all this is simply ignored by the Israeli public. Many of the findings mentioned here have been known for decades. The professional literature in the spheres of archaeology, Bible and the history of the Jewish people has addressed them in dozens of books and hundreds of articles. Even if not all the scholars accept the individual arguments that inform the examples I have cited, the majority have adopted their main points. Nevertheless, these revolutionary views are not penetrating the public consciousness. About a year ago, my colleague, the historian Prof. Nadav Ne'eman, published an article in the Culture and Literature section of Ha'aretz entitled 'To Remove the Bible from the Jewish Bookshelf', but there was no public outcry. Any attempt to question the reliability of the biblical descriptions is perceived as an attempt to undermine 'our historic right to the land' and as a shattering of the myth of the nation that is renewing the ancient Kingdom of Israel. These symbolic elements constitute such a critical component of the construction of the Israeli identity that any attempt to call their veracity into question encounters hostility or silence. It is of some interest that such tendencies within the Israeli secular society go hand-in-hand with the outlook among educated Christian groups. I have found a similar hostility in reaction to lectures I have delivered abroad to groups of Christian Bible lovers, though what upset them was the challenge to the foundations of their fundamentalist religious belief. It turns out that part of Israeli society is ready to recognize the injustice that was done to the Arab inhabitants of the country and is willing to accept the principle of equal rights for women - but is not up to adopting the archaeological facts that shatter the biblical myth. The blow to the mythical foundations of the Israeli identity is apparently too threatening, and it is more convenient to turn a blind eye.

Prof. Ze'ev Herzog teaches in the Department of Archaeology and Ancient Near Eastern Studies at Tel Aviv University. He took part in the excavations of Hazor and Megiddo with Yigael Yadin and in the digs at Tel Arad and Tel Be'er Sheva with Yohanan Aharoni. He has conducted digs at Tel Michal and Tel Gerisa and has recently begun digging at Tel Yaffo. He is the author of books on the city gate in Palestine and its neighbors and on two excavations, and has written a book summing up the archaeology of the ancient city.

EXCERPTS[35]

October 24, 1915. (Correspondence with A. Henry McMahon)

…. Subject to the above modifications, Great Britain is prepared to recognise and support the independence of the Arabs in all the regions within the limits demanded by the Sherif of Mecca.

November 2nd, 1917 (Balfour Declaration)

"His Majesty's Government view with favour the establishment in Palestine of a national home for the Jewish people, and will use their best endeavours to facilitate the achievement of this object, it being clearly understood that nothing shall be done which may prejudice the civil and religious rights of existing non-Jewish communities in Palestine, or the rights and political status enjoyed by Jews in any other country."

June, 15, 1922 (White Paper – Churchill)

…." In this connection it has been observed with satisfaction that at a meeting of the Zionist Congress, the supreme governing body of the Zionist Organization, held at Carlsbad in September, 1921, a resolution was passed expressing as the official statement of Zionist aims "the determination of the Jewish people to live with the Arab people on terms of unity and mutual respect, and together with them to make the common home into a flourishing community, the upbuilding of which may assure to each of its peoples an undisturbed national development."

---

[35] http://avalon.law.yale.edu/subject_menus/mideast.asp

PRESS RELEASE

August 2013
e-mail: almvillabooks@gmail.com
Tel. : 718-598-1183C
Website: www.almvillabooks.weebly.com

A Journey from a childhood in Nazi Germany to a love for Israel and Palestine and a deep desire for peace in the Middle East

Inge Etzbach announces the publication of her latest book, called "Bitter Harvest in the Promised Land – Myths, History and Conflict".   In her desire to understand and deal with the Holocaust and prevent this kind of inhumanity from ever happening again, she was preoccupied all her life with the desire to understand the complex issues at work in an area that call for reason and compassion and a careful balance between the longing of one's soul and the need to consider the souls and lives of others. She examines the core issues, the biblical myths, underlying assumptions and paradigms which helped shape Zionism and the State of Israel today and allows the suppression of another people, the Palestinians. The book also deals with the excavations and newest discoveries regarding the historical development of the people and the religion, and is influenced by the prophetic words of the people who try to find ways to heal the wounds of their country and its inhabitants.

"Goes to the core of the issues. Very informative and extremely important."

"Very powerful!"

"May your efforts help on the path to peace".

"I appreciate the light you throw on the issues".

Inge Etzbach was born in Germany one year before Hitler came to power and had the defining moment of her life when, only 12 years old, she saw concentration camp inmates at the end of the war. After the death of her husband, Inge lived for some time in Israel and the West Bank, worked in a Kibbutz , cleaned Uzi guns as a Volunteer for Israel on an army base, traveled through Israel and did research at the Truman Institute for the Advancement of Peace at Hebrew University in Jerusalem. She earned degrees in Philosophy and Political Science and is an ordained Interfaith Minister.

The book is available from amazon.com at $12.95

ISBN-13: 978-1470026967 ISBN-10: 1470026961

TIMELINE

1900 BCE	Abraham	Enters Canaan, Promised Land,	
1600-1550 BCE	Late Bronze Age Canaan culture	Amarna 1400-1350, Merenptah 1213-1203, Ugaritic tablet mentions Israelites in semitic script	
1400-1200 BCE	Canaan under Egyptian control		**Yahweh place-name in Sinai about Shasu people (1375 BCE)**
1300 BCE-1100 BCE	Late Bronze/Early Iron Age Fall of Canaan	Great Mycenean drought, settlements in Judean hills, proto-israel, Exodus from Egypt	
1025 – 926BCE	United Monarchy of Israel	Saul, David, Salomon	**Salomon erecting altars for strange gods**

950BCE	Iron Age	Assyrian denomination, Samaria (Israel) falls 722 BCE, Mesha stele,	
900 BCE	Israelite excavation site Tel Rehov near Jordan Valley	Only 2 external sources mention Israel up to this point (Merenptah and Mesha stele), nothing about the Davidian monarchy	**Signs of polytheistic worship**
835-800		Strong Israelite existence	
800 BCE	Near Hebron and the Sinai		**"Yahweh and his Asherah"**
700 BCE	Tel Dan	Stele mentioning "House of David"	
600 BCE	Jerusalem	Capital of Judea	**Silver amulet with name of Yahweh in Hebrew**
681 BCE	Niniveh library destroyed		
585 BCE	Babylonian Exile	State of Judea falls with Jerusalem	**Rise of Judaic Monotheism**
539 BCE	Exiles return	Babylon Falls	
539BCE	Persian Period	Cyrus the Great	**Early beginnings of**

			biblical traditions
300 BCE	Hellenistic Period	Greek translations, Dead Sea Scrolls	**Pentateuch versions and earliest biblical scrolls**
63 BCE	Roman Period		
132-135 CE	Bar Kochba's rebellion	Masada, Exile	
50-500 CE	Talmudic Traditions		**Talmud** **Consolidation of Judaism as a Religion**

DEFINITIONS

Israel	The State of Israel, proclaimed in 1948 as a homeland for the Jews living in the diaspora. Israelis are citizens of the State of Israel
Zionism	An international movement originally for the establishment of a Jewish national or religious community in Palestine and later for the support of modern Israel
Jews	Jews are an ethnoreligious group and include those born Jewish and converts to Judaism.
Fundamentalism	Defined as a movement or attitude stressing strict and literal adherence to a set of basic principles. In Judaism it is an attempt to go back to a situation which existed in Jewish communities before the advent of modernity.
Bible – Torah	The Torah is the Jewish name for the first five books of the Jewish Bible: Genesis, Exodus, Leviticus, Numbers and Deuteronomy.
Talmud	The Talmud ("instruction, learning") is a central text of mainstream Judaism. It takes the form of a record of rabbinic discussions pertaining to Jewish law, ethics, philosophy, customs and history
Midrash	The Interpretive Tradition of Torah
Mishna,	Collection of Jewish Oral Laws
Halakha	The legal part of Talmudic literature, an interpretation of the laws of the Scriptures
Palestine	Palestine is a geographical region in the Middle East. Based on the borders of Mandatory Palestine, the region today comprising primarily Israel, the Palestinian Authority, the Gaza Strip and small parts of Jordan. First mentioned as Philistia, an Iron Age pentapolis in the Southern Levant, established by Philistines c.1175 BC and existing in various forms until the Assyrian conquest in 8th century
Palestinians	Population of Palestine, also called "Arab"

RESOURCES

Atzmon, Gilad

 The Wandering Who?

Beker, Avi

 The Chosen

Barclay, J.M.G.

 Jews in the Mediterranean Diaspora

Beinart, Peter

 The Crisis of Zionism

Bennis, Phyllis

 Understanding the Palestinian-Israeli Conflict

Burg, Avraham

 The Holocaust is over – We must rise from its Ashes

Dever, William G.

 Who were the Early Israelites and Where did they come from?

Ellis, Marc H.

 Out of the Ashes

Entine, Jon

 Abrahm's Children: Race, Identity, and the DNA of the Chosen People

Finkelstein, Israel and Silberman, Neil Asher

>The Bible Unearthed

Finkelstein, Norman G.

>The Holocaust Industry

Friedman, Richard Elliott

>Who Wrote The Bible?

Goldstein, David B.

>Jacob's Legacy: A Genetic View of Jewish History

Herzberg, Arthur

>The Jews – The History and Character of a People

Jacobs, Louis

>A Jewish Theology

Kovel, Joel

>Overcoming Zionism

Neumann, Michael

>The Case Against Israel

Peled, Miko

>The General's Son

Rose, John

>The Myths of Zionism

Rosen, Brant

>Wrestling in the Daylight

Sacks, Rabbi Jonathan

To Heal a Fractured World

Sand, Shlomo

The Invention of the Jewish People

Shahak, Israel and Mezvinsky, Norton

Jewish Fundamentalism in Israel

Shahak, Israel

Jewish History Jewish Religion

Shipler, David K.

Arab and Jew

Smith, Mark S.

The Early History of God

Sturgiss, Mathew

Investigating the Truth of the Biblical Past

Thompson, Thomas L.

The Mythic Past

Whitelam, Keith W.

The Invention of Ancient Israel

Miles, Jack

God: A Biography

Robert Wright

The Evolution of God